TABLE OF CONTENTS

DIGNITARIES,

NEAR AND FAR

SPICED ROAST CHICKEN

1 (3 1/2 lb.) chicken
1 T. margarine
2/3 c. Marsala
<u>Mushroom Stuffing:</u>
2 T. olive oil
1 onion, finely chopped
1 tsp. Garam Masala (optional)
4 oz. button or brown mushrooms, chopped
1 c. coarsely grated parsnips
1 c. coarsely grated carrots
1/4 c. minced walnuts
2 tsps. chopped fresh thyme
1 c. fresh white bread crumbs
1 egg, beaten
Salt and pepper to taste

Preheat Oven to 375° (109C).
<u>Prepare Stuffing:</u> In a large saucepan, heat olive oil; add onion and sauté two minutes or until softened. Stir in garam masala and cook one minute. Add mushrooms, parsnips and carrots; cook, stirring five minutes. Remove from heat; stir in remaining ingredients.
Stuff and truss chicken. Place, breast side down, in a roasting pan; add 1/4 cup water. Roast 45 minutes; turn chicken breast up and dot with margarine. Roast about 45 minutes more or until a meat thermometer inserted in the thickest part of the thigh (not touching the bone) registers 185° (85C). Transfer to a platter and keep warm.
Pour off and discard fat from roasting pan; add Marsala to remaining cooking juices, stirring to scrape up any browned bits. Boil over high heat one minute to reduce slightly and adjust seasoning.
Garnish with thyme and watercress sprigs. Serve with seasonal vegetables.
Makes 4 servings.

Office of the Vice-President of the United States,
Al Gore

BEEF STEW

4 lbs. beef chuck, cut into 1 1/2" cubes
1 bunch celery, cut into 1" pieces
1 1/2 lbs. whole, peeled baby carrots
2 lbs. whole, peeled small potatoes
1 15oz. can stewed tomatoes
1 quart beef stock
1 cup pearl onions
1 cup frozen peas
1/2 cup oil
3/4 cup flour
Salt & pepper
3 bay leaves

Season beef with salt and pepper. In a large, heavy saucepan, sear the beef in oil until well browned. Remove and reserve.
Add pearl onions and allow to brown, remove and reserve.
Add celery pieces and brown edges, remove and reserve.
Add flour to remaining oil and make a roux. Brown slightly, stirring often.
Add half of the stock and blend with the roux until smooth. Add the remaining stock and bring to a boil.
Add bay leaves, beef and tomatoes with juice. Return to a boil. Lower the heat to simmer. Cover and cook until meat is very tender.
Add carrots, potatoes, celery and onions. Simmer for an additional 20 to 30 minutes until potatoes are tender. Adjust salt and pepper to taste. Remove bay leaves and discard. Degrease the stew. Add peas several moments before serving.

New York State Governor,
George E. Pataki

(2)

PASTA WITH RICOTTA A LAFALCE

2 lbs. spinach
1 lb. fresh ricotta cheese
3 eggs, lightly beaten
2/3 cups grated Parmesan cheese
1/3 cups chopped parsley, preferably Italian
2 tsp. salt
1/2 tsp. freshly ground pepper
4 cups marinara sauce
1 lb. tube-like pasta (ziti or penne)

Preheat oven to 375°. Pick over spinach, trimming away and discarding tough stems. Rinse the leaves well and drain. Cook spinach briefly, tightly covered, in the water that clings to the leaves. Stir the spinach as it cooks just until the leaves are wilted. Drain well in a colander. When the spinach is cool enough to handle, press it to remove most of the moisture and chop.
Combine the cooked spinach, ricotta, eggs and Parmesan cheese, parsley, salt, pepper and marinara sauce. Blend.
Bring a large quantity of water to a boil and add the pasta, stirring rapidly. Cook, stirring, for two minutes, then drain the pasta in a colander and add to the ricotta mixture. Pour the mixture into a baking dish and bake 25 to 30 minutes, or until the pasta is tender but not mushy. Do not overcook! Serve with additional parmesan cheese on the side. Serves six to eight.

Congressman,
John J. LaFalce

HOUSE OF REPRESENTATIVES
WASHINGTON, D. C. 20515

CHICKEN SOUP

32 oz. can chicken broth
32 oz. cold water
1 whole chicken (with the insides removed)
1 1/2 cups celery, chopped
1 1/2 cups carrots, chopped
1 medium onion, chopped fine
2 Tbsp. parsley
Salt & pepper to taste

After bringing the chicken broth, water and chicken to a boil, add all other ingredients. After approximately 10 minutes, turn the heat down and simmer for one hour. At this time, remove the chicken and let it cool. Remove the meat from the bones and add it back into the soup.
A quick and easy recipe for a delicious meal!
Option: Cook and add any type noodle or white rice to add variation.

New York State Senator,
George D. Maziarz

BAVARIAN APPLE TORT

Group I:
1/2 cup butter or margarine
1/4 cup sugar
1/4 tsp. vanilla
1 cup flour
Group II:
16 oz. cream cheese
1/2 cup sugar
2 eggs
1 tsp. vanilla
Group III:
1/2 cup sugar with 1 tsp. cinnamon
2 1/2 cups apples, peeled & sliced
1/4 cup almonds, sliced

(con't)

BAVARIAN APPLE TORT (con't)

From group I, cream butter and sugar, add vanilla and blend in flour. Spread dough onto bottom and sides of a 9" spring form pan. Combine all ingredients from group II mixing well. Pour into dough-lined pan. Combine ingredients from group III, except almonds. Put over the cream cheese mixture and sprinkle with the almonds. Bake at 450° for 10 minutes. Reduce heat to 400° and bake for 30 minutes. Cool, slice and serve. This may also be baked in a 9" by 13" pan.

Wright H. Ellis,
Supervisor, Town of Cambria

CHILI MY WAY

1 can red kidney beans	1 cube beef bouillon
1 large onion, chopped	1 1/2 tsp. salt
1 lb. ground beef	Dash paprika
2 Tbsp. fat	3 whole cloves
2 cans tomatoes (3 1/2 cups)	2 tsp. chili powder
1 can tomato paste (small)	1 Tbsp. sugar
2 Tbsp. chili sauce	1 cup celery, chopped

Brown onion and ground beef in hot fat. Add tomatoes, paste and seasonings., Simmer two hours. Add water, if necessary. Add celery and kidney beans. Cook 15 minutes. Serves 6.

Richard F. Demus,
Supervisor, Town of Lewiston

ITALIAN BAKED MUSHROOMS

3 lbs. mushrooms
3 Tbsp. parsley, chopped
1 clove garlic, sliced
3/4 cup bread crumbs
1/4 cup grated cheese

1 tsp. salt
1 tsp. pepper
1 tsp. oregano
1/4 cup oil
1/4 cup bouillon

Prepare mushrooms. Place in a buttered dish. Sprinkle with seasonings. Cover with half of the crumbs and cheese and pour on the oil. Add rest of the crumbs and cheese. Bake 40 to 45 minutes at 350°. Add bouillon 15 minutes before done if they appear too dry.

J.O. Thompson,
Supervisor, Town of Lockport

EGG BRAID BREAD

2 cups milk, scalded
2 Tbsp. sugar
2 tsp. salt
2 Tbsp. shortening
2 eggs, lightly beaten
1 pkg. dry yeast
1/4 cup warm water
5 to 7 cups flour

Pour milk (hot) over sugar, salt & shortening. Cool to lukewarm.
Soften yeast in water. Add yeast and eggs to milk mixture. Beat in flour, one cup at a time. Knead five to ten minutes. Let rise to double size. Shapes into six ropes (15 inches long) and braid into two loaves. Let rise on greased cookie sheet. Brush loaves with another egg beaten with 1 Tbsp. cold water and dust with sesame seeds.
Bake at 375° for 25 minutes.

John Hayden,
Mayor - Barker Village

BEST STICKY BUNS

2 Tbsp. soft shortening
2 Tbsp. sugar
1 tsp. salt
1 egg, beaten
1/2 cup warm mashed potatoes
1 pkg. yeast in 1 cup warm water
3 cups white flour (+ or -)

Mix and knead for five minutes until smooth and elastic. Refrigerate overnight.
Roll out dough into a rectangle and butter well with melted butter. Sprinkle with cinnamon and sugar. In a glass baking pan place one cup maple syrup, 1/2 cup water and a few chopped nuts. Roll the dough in a jellyroll fashion and slice into one inch slices. Place slices, sides down, into a 9" by 15" baking dish to rise.
When doubled, bake at 350° for 30 minutes. When done, turn out on a baking rack to cool. Good Eating!

John Hayden,
Mayor, Barker Village

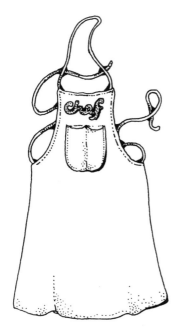

FETTUCINE ALFREDO FOR TWO

1/2 lb. fettuccine noodles
1 pt. heavy cream
1/4 lb. butter
1 to 2 tsp. garlic, chopped
2 Tbsp. Romano cheese
2 Tbsp. Parmesan cheese
Dash of parsley & white pepper

Cook fettuccine until aldente, rinse in cold water and drain. To make white sauce: Sauté butter and garlic, add heavy cream. Boil until reduced; slightly add cheeses and stir until melted. Mix in cooked fettuccine with dash of parsley and white pepper until blended.
Fettuccine DeFlippo: Same recipe as above but add 1/4 lb. small, cooked shrimp and 1/2 cup chopped clams before adding fettuccine to the sauce.
Optional: Add 3 oz. dry, white wine to the white sauce.

Gerald DeFlippo,
Niagara County Legislator

SHRIMP DIP

1 8oz. pkg. of cream cheese
1 1/2 pt. sour cream
1 can shrimp or small fresh, cooked shrimp
1 onion, minced
1/2 tsp. garlic (2 cloves, minced)
Salt & pepper to taste

Soften cream cheese and mix with sour cream. Mix the rest of the ingredients and bake at 350° for 1/2 hour.
Serve with crackers or chips.

Bradley Erck,
Niagara County Legislator

PARMESAN PUFFS

2 cups mayonnaise
1 cup Parmesan cheese
1 onion, grated
hotdog rolls (unsliced, bakery style)

Slice hotdog rolls in 1/2" rounds. Put 1/2 tsp. mixture on each round. Place on a cookie sheet and broil in oven until brown and bubbly.

FRUIT DIP

1 can (8oz) crushed pineapple with juice
3 oz. pkg. of instant coconut pudding
3/4 cup milk
1/2 cup sour cream

Blend all ingredients together for 30 seconds.

Bradley Erck,
Niagara County Legislator

SUGAR COOKIES

1 cup shortening
2 cups sugar (1brown & 1 white)
2 eggs
1 cup buttermilk
1 tsp. baking soda
2 tsp. baking powder
1/2 tsp. salt
4 cups flour
Nutmeg & cinnamon

(con't next page)

SUGAR COOKIES (CON'T)

Mix shortening and sugar together. Add eggs and beat until fluffy. Add the rest of the ingredients and flavor with nutmeg and cinnamon to taste.

Chill (freeze for two hours is best). Roll out on a floured board. Cut out shapes and bake at 425° to 450° for six minutes.

Lee Simonson,
Niagara County Legislator

BROCCOLI SALAD

1 bunch broccoli, cut up small
1 medium onion, diced
1/2 lb. bacon, fried, drained & crumbled (or 1/4 c. bacon bits)
1/2 cup cheddar cheese, shredded
1/2 cup mayonnaise or salad dressing
1/4 cup sugar
1 Tbsp. vinegar

Mix together and refrigerate.

LEMON ANGEL FOOD CAKE

1 angel food cake
1 box regular lemon pudding
Coconut

Cook one box (reg. size) lemon pudding by the directions on the box. Slice the cake into 3 layers. Spread the pudding between layers, saving some for the top. Sprinkle with coconut. Can be served with whipped cream if desired. Chill several hours before serving.

Lorraine Wayner,
Historian, Towns of Barker & Somerset

LAYERED CHEF SALAD

In a salad bowl, place in layers the following:
1 head of lettuce-shredded
A few leaves of spinach
1 cup diced celery
1 cup chopped green pepper
1 cup chopped sweet onion
1 pkg. frozen peas, cooked & drained - placed on top

Spread on top:
1 cup mayonnaise

Sprinkle over all:
3 Tbsp. sugar
Bacon bits to taste
Grated cheddar cheese - to cover

Marinate overnight.   Serve as above.   Do not stir!
Very attractive if prepared in glass or plastic bowl.

SNACK TIME MOLASSES COOKIES

1 1/c. flour
3/4 tsp. baking soda
1/2 tsp. salt
1/2 cup butter or margarine
3/4 cup sugar

1 egg, unbeaten
¼ cup molasses
1 cup coconut
1 cup raisins

Combine flour, soda and salt and set aside. Cream butter and sugar and mix well with the egg and molasses. Combine with the dry ingredients.
Drop onto greased cookie sheets and bake at 375° for 8 to 10 minutes.

Lorraine G. Wayner,
Historian, Towns of Barker & Somerset
(11)

PEANUT BUTTER PIE

1 8oz. pkg. cream cheese, softened
1 1/2 cups plus 3 Tbsp. confectioners sugar
1 cup peanut butter
1 cup milk
6oz. container of cool whip.

Beat cream cheese, sugar and peanut butter together until well blended. Slowly add 1 cup milk and blend. Fold in cool whip and place mixture in a 10" pie shell. Freeze overnight.

Anna B. Wallace,
Historian, Village of Middleport

CANDIED BRAZIL NUT LOG

1 lb. brazil nuts
1 lb. dates, pitted
3/4 lb. candied cherries
1 lb. candied pineapple
3/4 cup sifted flour
3/4 cup sugar
1/2 tsp. baking powder
3 eggs
1 tsp. vanilla
Salt

Combine dates, nuts, cherries and pineapple in a large bowl. Sift flour, sugar, baking powder and salt and mix with the fruit. Beat eggs until foamy. Add vanilla.
Add this mixture to the nut, fruit, flour mixture. Mix very well. Pack in two greased, waxed paper lined one quart molds. Bake in a slow oven 300° for one hour and 45 minutes. Remove from pan and tear off paper.

Donald E. Loker,
Historian, City of Niagara Falls

SOFT SUGAR COOKIES

2/3 cup shortening
1 1/2 cups white sugar
2 eggs
2 tsp. vanilla
1 cup sour cream
4 to 4 1/2 cups flour

1 tsp. baking powder
1 tsp. baking soda
1 tsp. salt
Nutmeg
Raisins

Sift flour, baking powder, baking soda, salt and nutmeg to taste and set aside. Beat shortening and sugar, then add eggs and vanilla. Mix with dry ingredients and add raisins as desired.
Roll out about 1/4" thick. Place on a greased cookie sheet and sprinkle with white sugar. Bake at 375° for eight minutes.

Donald Jerge,
Historian, Town of Royalton

TRADITIONAL BAKED BEANS

1 lb. navy beans
1 small onion, chopped
1/2 cup molasses
4 oz. salt pork (bacon or ham)

1 cup water
1 tsp. dry mustard
Salt & pepper

Cover the beans with water and soak overnight. Rinse, cover with fresh water and simmer for about two hours. Place the beans, pork and onion in a casserole dish. Mix the mustard, molasses, salt and pepper with the one cup of water and stir into the bean mixture. If the liquid does not just cover the beans, add a little water.
Bake in a moderate oven (375°) for about two hours. Remove the pork, break into pieces and return to the bean mixture before serving. This recipe can be made at home and warmed up in camp, or adapted to cook it right in camp!

Tom & Ruth Beecher,
Niagara's Own Co.H of the 49th NYVI,
Civil War Reenactment Assoc.

FRIED PIES

Stew two cups dried apples, apricots or peaches in water until tender. Drain and mash. Add sugar to taste. If available, add cinnamon, allspice, nutmeg or lemon peel to your taste.

Using biscuit dough or flaky pie pastry (3 cups flour, 1 tsp. salt, 1 1/3 cups lard or butter and lard, and ice cold water; mix, roll and fold over several times), make small balls and roll out thinly to the size of a saucer. Spoon some apples or other fruit into the center of each piece of dough. Moisten the edge of the dough with water and fold into a half-moon shape. Crimp the edges together with a fork and fry each pie in hot grease in a skillet, turning to brown each side.

RABBIT STEW

1 rabbit, dressed and cut into pieces*	Mixed herbs (saffron, basil, marjoram, thyme, parsley or poultry seasoning)
Salt & pepper	
4 Tbsp. butter	
3/4 cup chopped carrots	1 1/2 cups water
1 cup coarsely chopped potato	2 chopped onions

Mix the flour and seasonings together, and coat the rabbit in the mixture. Melt the butter and fry the rabbit pieces to brown. Put the pieces in a large pan and add the onion, carrot, and potato. Cover with water and season with salt, pepper and herbs. Cover and cook in a moderate oven (375°) for about one hour.

* If rabbit "looks like chicken, tastes like chicken", use chicken!

Tom & Ruth Beecher,
Niagara's Own Co. H of the 49th NYVI,
Civil War Reenactment Assoc.

RECIPES & NOTES

RECIPES & NOTES

BAKERIES

&

RESTAURANTS

PUMPKIN PIE

1 1/4 cup flour	1 1/2 tsp. cinnamon
1/2 tsp. salt (for crust)	1/2 tsp.cloves
6 Tbsp. shortening	1/2 tsp. allspice
1 cup sugar (part brown,	1/2 tsp. nutmeg
part white)	1/2 tsp. ginger
2 eggs, beaten	1/2 tsp. salt (for filling)
1 1/2 cups cooked and mashed pumpkin	
1 large can evaporated milk	

Cut shortening into flour and salt with pastry blender. Sprinkle with three to four Tbsp. cold water, one Tbsp. at a time. Gather together and roll out to fit 10" pie plate. Do not stretch but ease in gently. Allow 1/2" to overhang and turn under. Flute edges.
Filling: Blend together sugar, spices, eggs, pumpkin and milk. Pour into pie shell and bake in 400° oven for one hour or until custard is set.

RASPBERRY CRUMBLE COFFEE CAKE

Filling:

1 cup raspberries, crushed	2 Tbsp. cornstarch
1 cup raspberries, whole	1 tsp. lemon juice
1/2 cup water	1/2 cup sugar

Combine crushed berries, water, cornstarch and sugar and cook over medium heat until thickened and clear. Add lemon juice and fold in the whole berries. Let cool.

Cake:

1 1/2 cups flour	1/8 tsp. mace
1/2 cup sugar	1/2 cup butter
1 1/2 tsp. baking powder	1 egg
1/2 tsp. salt	1/2 cup milk
1/2 tsp. cinnamon	1/2 tsp. vanilla

(con't next page)

RASPBERRY CRUMBLE COFFEE CAKE (con't)

Sift together dry ingredients. Add butter and cut in as for pie crust to make fine crumbs. Add egg, milk and vanilla and stir until blended. Spread half of batter in buttered round 8" pan. Spread cooled filling over top and then drop remaining batter by small spoonfuls over filling and spread.

Topping:
1/2 cup flour   1/4 cup butter
1/2 cup sugar   1/4 cup almonds, sliced

Combine flour and sugar. Cut in the butter and stir in almonds. Sprinkle over top of coffee cake.
Bake in 350° oven for 40 to 45 minutes, or until cake tests done in center and is golden on top. Allow to cool in pan. Sift with confectioners sugar.
Recipe may be doubled and baked in 13" by 9" by 2" pan for 45 to 50 minutes.

STRAWBERRY PIZZA

Crust:
1 1/2 cups flour   1/4 cup brown sugar
1 cup butter   1/2 cup chopped pecans
                              or almonds

Filling:
1 8oz. pkg. cream cheese   2/3 cup powdered sugar
1 9oz.container whipped topping

Topping:
1 3oz.pkg. strawberry jello   Dash salt
1/2 cup sugar   4 Tbsp. cornstarch
4 cups sliced strawberries   1 cup water or strawberry
                                  juice, divided

(con't next page)

STRAWBERRY PIZZA (CON'T)

Crust: Mix all ingredients to form dough and spread in pizza pan. Bake at 375° for 15 minutes.

Filling: Mix cream cheese and powdered sugar and fold in whipped topping. Spread on cooled crust.

Topping: Combine jello, sugar, salt and 1/2 cup water or juice. Dissolve cornstarch in remaining 1/2 cup of liquid and stir into gelatin mixture. Cook over medium heat until thickened. Stir in strawberries to coat all slices. Cool and spread on top of filling. Chill. Cut in wedges to serve. Top with whipped cream (optional).

The three preceding recipes were submitted by
Ruth Jerge of Becker Farms, Gasport,
and were made on AM Buffalo, Channel 7

PIZZA RUSTICA

2 1lb. pieces DiCamillo bread dough

2 12oz. jars roasted sweet red peppers

3 8oz. pkgs. frozen spinach

1/4 lb. sliced Capac olla

1/4 lb. shredded mozz. or Fontanella cheese

1/4 lb grated Parmesan cheese

1/4 lb. grated Romano cheese

1 can pitted black olives, drained

1 jar green salad olives, drained

1 chopped green onion

1 chopped clove garlic

2 Tbsp. olive oil

1 egg, beaten with 1 Tbsp. water (egg wash)

1 oz. sesame seeds

Salt & pepper to taste

Defrost spinach and drain well. Add garlic, onion, 1 Tbsp. oil, salt and pepper, and place in a food processor or hand chop to a puree.

Drain peppers and place in a small bowl, adding remaining oil.

(cont' next page)

(17)

PIZZA RUSTICA (CON'T)

Roll out one pound of dough very thinly on a lightly floured surface. Place dough in bottom of greased 8" spring form pan so that bottom and sides are covered with an overhang of dough.

Cover bottom of pan with layer of Capac olla. Generously layer roasted peppers and sprinkle with the Romano and parmesan cheese. Spread part of the spinach mixture on top of cheese. Add a layer of Fontanella or Mozzarella, then a layer of green and black olives. Repeat layers until the ingredients are used up and pan is full.

Roll out remaining one pound of dough until thin. Brush with egg wash and place over pan of ingredients. Cut off excess and seal edges. Use excess dough to roll out two 14" cords and braid. Dip dough braid in egg wash and arrange around the edge of the pizza. Sprinkle with sesame seeds. Slit the top to allow steam to escape.

Bake 45 minutes in a preheated 400° oven or until crust is golden brown. Remove from oven; remove spring form ring. Brush sides with egg wash, cover top with foil and put pizza back in oven to brown sides.

Serve cold with fresh green salad for lunch or as a dinner appetizer.

DiCamillo Bakery,
Niagara Falls & Lewiston

SPECIAL LASAGNA

2 chicken breasts, boned
4 thin slices Prosciutto (dry spiced Italian ham)
3 lbs. ground beef
5 lbs. ricotta cheese
3 Tbsp. Romano cheese
3 Tbsp. Parmesan cheese
4 eggs
1 small onion, minced
3 #2 1/2 cans tomatoes
1 #2 1/2 can tomato puree
1 lb. lasagna noodles
Salt, pepper, parsley, garlic powder, sugar,
    crushed sweet basil

Brown ground beef. Start cooking tomatoes and puree; season to taste with salt, garlic, sugar, parsley and basil. Remove two cups of sauce and set aside to use with chicken. Add the rest of the sauce with the beef.
Dice chicken breasts into two inch pieces. In a large frying pan, sauté the chicken and onion in oil. Season to taste with salt, pepper, garlic and brown. Transfer into saucepan and add the two cups of saved sauce. Let cook until tender (20-25 minutes). Mix ricotta cheese, eggs, salt, pepper, garlic and parsley. Dice Prosciutto and add to cheese mixture with Romano and Parmesan cheeses.
Cook noodles al dente in salt water.
Layer as follows: meat sauce in bottom, then layer of noodles, then cheese mixture, then noodles, then chicken in sauce, then noodles, then cover with the rest of the meat sauce.
Bake 350° for 20 to 25 minutes. Serves 15.

From the recipe book of Gerald R. DeFlippo,
DeFlippo's Restaurant

CRAB STUFFED HADDOCK

2 lbs. fresh haddock, skinless (four pieces)
1 1/2 sticks butter
1/4 green pepper, chopped fine
1/4 red pepper, chopped fine
1 small onion, chopped fine
2 oz. chicken base
1/2 lb. artificial crab meat
1/2 lb. Korean crab meat
1 cup Japanese flakes
1 cup Monterey jack cheese
Garlic powder, cayenne pepper

Sauté butter, green pepper, red pepper and onion. Add chicken base and crab meats. Cook down and add Japanese flakes and garlic and pepper to taste. Let cool and add cheese.
Take skinless pieces of haddock and flatten. Spoon crab stuffing onto larger ends and roll up. Place in pan and bake at 400° for 20 minutes. When almost done cover each roll of fish with one slice of provolone cheese. When melted, serve. Serves four.

PEANUT BUTTER PIE

1 pie shell (baked)

Melt over low heat:
12 oz. chocolate chips
1/2 stick butter
Pour into pie shell and spread over surface in thin layer, saving a small amount to drizzle over finished pie.

(con't next page)

PEANUT BUTTER PIE (CON'T)

Filling:
1 1/2 cups peanut butter
1 1/2 cups confectioners sugar
16 oz. whipped cream
Blend in mixing bowl and fill pie shell. Drizzle remaining chocolate over the top.
Refrigerate.

The two preceding recipes were submitted by
Brian & Charlene Bower, Proprietors,
Lock Side Cafe,
Lockport, NY

MEATBALLS

5 lbs. ground beef
9 eggs
3 cups seasoned bread crumbs
1 Tbsp. red crushed pepper
2 Tbsp. garlic powder
2 Tbsp. onion powder

Mix all ingredients and form into two inch meatballs. Preheat oven to 425°. Bake for 45 to 50 minutes or until between 160° and 180°.
Makes 80 to 100 meatballs.

Beth Shero,
Shero's Country Restaurant,
Lockport, NY

RECIPES & NOTES

BED

&

BREAKFASTS

Come Visit
The Niagara County
Historical Society, Inc.

and catch a glimpse of area life over the last 175
years, through its five building complex located at
215 Niagara St., Lockport, NY 14094
Some displays include: Victorian Music Room,
rooms on the Civil War, Toys and Dolls, Victorian
Pantry, Early American Trades, the Iroquois Indians,
the Erie Canal, Early Transportation and so much
more!

Outwater Emporium

A unique museum gift shop with a wide selection of
books pertaining to Niagara County, Young People's
Corner, Victorian and other gift items and a wide
selection of postcards and souvenirs.

The Col. William Bond House

143 Ontario St., Lockport, NY 14094
Enjoy walking through this 1924 National Register
home. Restored in the Empire Period are twelve
furnished rooms where history lives on!
Group tours for the museum complex and Bond
House with a guide or for current open hours
call (716) 434-7433

CINNAMON COFFEE CAKE

2 1/2 cups raisin bran flakes
2 1/2 cups flour
1 1/2 tsp. baking powder
1 1/2 cups plain low fat yogurt
6 egg whites
1 Tbsp. vanilla
1 Tbsp. cinnamon
1 cup light brown sugar
1 1/2 tsp. baking soda
1/2 cup skim milk
1/3 cup margarine, softened

Combine one cup of cereal and the cinnamon, crush lightly and set aside. Place remaining cereal in a large mixing bowl and crush lightly. Add flour, sugar, baking powder, baking soda and mix well. Add yogurt, milk, egg whites, margarine and vanilla to the flour mixture. Blend on low speed, then beat at medium speed for one minute. Pour 1 1/2 cups batter into a greased 12 cup bundt pan or tube pan. Sprinkle with half the cereal/cinnamon mixture. Cover with remaining batter, then remaining cereal.
Bake in preheated 350° oven for 35 to 40 minutes or until cake tester comes out clean. Cool in pan for five minutes. Turn out onto a rack. Serve warm, sprinkled with confectioners sugar if desired.

BAYSIDE GUEST HOUSE
Olcott, NY
Jane Voelpel, proprietor

SHREDDED WHEAT PANCAKES
Mix 2 eggs, well beaten, a pinch of salt, 1 cup milk in a bowl. Dip 6 shredded wheat biscuits in this mixture and fry in hot fat until golden brown. Serve with any good syrup.

TOMATO SLICES WITH GREEN SAUCE

1/2 cup dairy sour cream
1/4 cup finely chopped parsley
1/2 cup watercress, including stems
1/3 cup mayonnaise
2 whole scallions, chopped fine

Season to taste with lemon juice, salt and white pepper, then pour over two large sliced beefsteak tomatoes cut 1/2" thick.
Makes three to four servings.

THE COL. WILLIAM BOND HOUSE
Lockport, NY
(Even though the Bond House is not a B & B, this recipe was served many times at various functions held at the home. The Bond House is on the National Register and is owned by the NCHS, Inc.)

BLUEBERRY MUFFINS

1 1/2 cups sifted flour
2 tsp. baking powder
1/2 tsp. salt
1/2 cup sugar
1 egg, beaten
1/2 cup milk
1/4 cup melted butter
1 1/2 cups blueberries

Mix dry ingredients together. Add egg, milk and butter and mix until moistened. Fold in blueberries and put into buttered muffin tins. Sprinkle with mixture of 2 Tbsp. sugar and 1 tsp. lemon rind.
Bake at 375° for 20 to 25 minutes.

COUNTRY COTTAGE
Gasport, NY
Sue Pearson, Proprietress

MY MOM'S BISCUITS OR SHORTCAKE

2 cups flour
1/2 tsp. salt
1/2 stick butter or margarine
1 egg in a cup & fill with milk
4 tsp. baking powder
3 Tbsp. sugar

Sift dry ingredients, add butter then egg and milk. Divide and drop into eight, greased cupcake tins.
Bake 450° for ten minutes.
Note: for shortcake, add more sugar to batter.

THE FORMER NATIONAL CENTENNIAL HOUSE
Lockport, NY
Marvin & Billie Pascoe, Proprietors

APPLESAUCE MUFFINS

1 cup soft margarine
2 cups sugar
2 eggs
3 tsp. vanilla
4 cups flour
1 tsp. cloves

2 tsp. allspice
3 tsp. cinnamon
2 tsp. baking soda
2 cups applesauce
1/2 cup raisins
1/2 cup walnuts

Cream margarine, sugar, eggs and vanilla. Sift flour, spices and baking soda together. Add dry ingredients to creamed mixture. Mix in applesauce and stir well. Mill muffin cups half full.
Bake at 400° for 12 minutes. Makes 4 doz. muffins. Batter can be kept in refrigerator and baked as needed.

EVERGREEN FARM
Sanborn, NY
Wayne & Marcia Rivers, Proprietors

NIGHT BEFORE FRENCH TOAST

1 large loaf French bread   10 large eggs
3/4 tsp. salt   4 tsp. sugar
1 Tbsp. vanilla   3 cups milk
4 Tbsp. butter, cut in small pieces

Use Pam spray to grease 9" by 13" pan. Cut bread into one inch thick slices and arrange into single layer. Beat eggs with remaining ingredients except butter. When thoroughly mixed, pour over bread in pan. Cover with foil and refrigerate overnight.

Next morning, remove foil. Heat oven to 350° and dot with butter. Bake 45 minutes until bread is golden brown. Remove from oven and let sit for 5 minutes. Serve warm with powdered sugar, fresh fruit or yogurt. Serves six.

LINEN 'N LACE
Niagara Falls, NY
Mary Martin, proprietress

SCOTTISH OAT SCONES

2/3 cup melted butter or marg.   1/4 cup sugar
1/3 cup milk   1 Tbsp. baking powder
1 egg   1 tsp. cream of tartar
1 1/2 cups flour   ½ tsp. salt
1 1/4 cups rolled oats   ½ cup raisins

Combine butter, milk and egg. Combine rest of ingredients. Mix both together just until moistened. Shape into a ball. Pat out into eight inch circle on cookie sheet sprayed with Pam. Score into eight to twelve wedges.

Bake at 450° for 12 to 15 minutes.

RAISED WAFFLES

1/2 cup warm water (105-115°)
1 pkg. dry yeast
2 cups milk
1/2 cup melted butter
1 tsp. salt
1 tsp. sugar
2 cups flour
1/4 tsp. baking soda
2 eggs, room temperature

Pour warm water into a large mixing bowl. Sprinkle in the yeast. Let stand five minutes to dissolve. Warm the milk and butter until butter melts. Cool to lukewarm. Add milk, butter, salt, sugar and flour to yeast mixture. Beat until smooth and well blended. Cover bowl with plastic wrap and let stand at room temperature overnight.

When ready to cook waffles, beat in eggs, add baking soda and stir until well blended. The batter will be very thin. Cook in waffle iron.

The two preceding recipes were submitted by
MANCHESTER HOUSE
Niagara Falls, NY

ORANGE POPPYSEED BREAD

Beat until light:
1 cup sour cream   1/2 cup margarine
3/4 cup sugar

Add:
2 eggs   2 cups flour
1 Tbsp. poppy seed   1 tsp. baking soda
1 Tbsp. grated orange rind   1 tsp. baking powder
2 Tbsp. orange juice   1/2 tsp. salt

(con't next page)

ORANGE POPPYSEED BREAD (CON'T)

Beat at low speed until combined. Bake at 325° for 50 to 55 minutes. Makes one 9" by 5" loaf or three small mini loaves.

APPLE MUFFINS WITH SAUCE

Muffins:
1 Tbsp. butter
1 cup flour
1 tsp. baking soda
1/2 cup chopped nuts
1 cup brown sugar

1/8 tsp. salt
1 tsp. vanilla
1 egg
2 Tbsp. boiling water
1 cup tart apples, peeled & diced

Sauce:
1 cup brown sugar
4 Tbsp. butter
2 Tbsp. flour

1 tsp. vanilla
1/2 cup boiling water

Muffins: Combine all ingredients in order given. Pour batter in greased muffin tins filling them 2/3 full.
Bake at 350° for 20 to 25 minutes. While muffins are baking make sauce: Mix brown sugar and flour together in a small saucepan. Add the water, butter and vanilla. Cook over medium heat until thickened. Serve hot sauce over the muffins.

The two preceding recipes were submitted by
MAPLEHURST
Lockport, NY
Mark Herbst, Proprietor

SOFT OATMEAL RAISIN COOKIES

Cream together:
1 cup margarine, softened
3/4 cup brown sugar, packed
1/4 cup white sugar
2 eggs

Stir in:
1 4oz. pkg. instant vanilla pudding
1 tsp. baking soda
1 1/4 cups flour

Add:
3 1/2 cups quick rolled oats
1 cup raisins (soften by soaking in 1/4 cup boiling water,
    drain and cool before adding)
Drop by spoonfuls on ungreased cookie sheet and bake at 375°
for 10 to 12 minutes.

RAINBOW GUEST HOUSE
Niagara Falls, NY
LauraLee & Frank Sneller, Hosts
Jeffrey Houk, manager

TEA COOLERS ~ORANGE & CREAM

1/4 cup Lipton 100% instant tea
1/2 cup water
1 cup vanilla ice cream
1 1/2 cups orange juice

In blender, combine all ingredients. Process at high speed until
thoroughly blended. Pour into glasses. Makes four servings.

WHEELER'S GUEST HOUSE
Wilson, NY
Howard & Hannelore Wheeler, Proprietors

RECIPES & NOTES

RECIPES & NOTES

APPETIZERS

&

BEVERAGES

PINEAPPLE DIP

1 4 1/2 oz. can of deviled ham
1 3 oz. pkg. cream cheese
3/4 cup crushed pineapple

Blend ham and cream cheese. Drain pineapple reserving the juice. Combine pineapple with ham and cream cheese adding just enough juice for dip consistency. Let stand at room temperature for 15 minutes before serving, preferably overnight. Store in covered container in refrigerator.

Clara Lockie

SHRIMP DIP

1 can shrimp, drained and washed
1 8oz. pkg. cream cheese, softened
2 Tbsp. horseradish
2 Tbsp. ketchup
Dash Tabasco, optional

Mix together well. Chill and serve with crackers.

Joan Pearson

SHRIMP DIP

1 8oz. pkg. cream cheese
1/4 cup mayonnaise
2 Tbsp. onion, chopped fine
1 to 2 Tbsp. ketchup
1 4 1/2 oz. pkg. shrimp or crabmeat

Beat first four ingredients at medium speed, then add shrimp and beat on low. Chill and serve.

Virginia Strablow

DERRI THOMAS' CRAB DIP

1 can crabmeat
1/4 cup chili sauce
1/4 cup salad dressing
3 Tbsp. onion, grated

Mix and chill.   Serve on crackers.

Melissa Dunlap

SCOTCH OAT CRACKERS
Grind or crush 2 cups rolled oats and mix with
1/4 cup milk, 1/4 cup molasses, 1 1/2 Tbsp. fat,
1/4 tsp. soda and 1 tsp. salt. Roll out in a thin
sheet and cut in squares.
Bake for 20 minutes in a moderate oven.

HOT CRABMEAT SPREAD

1 8 oz. pkg. imitation crab
1 8 oz. pkg. cream cheese
2 to 3 Tbsp. minced onion (Vidalia is best)
1 Tbsp. milk
1 to 2 Tbsp. horseradish
Dash salt
1/4 cup slivered almonds
parsley

Combine all ingredients except almonds and parsley.   Beat
until well mixed.   Spread in an ungreased casserole dish.
Sprinkle with almonds, then parsley.
Bake at 350° for 20 minutes. Serve with crackers.

Maggie Lupo

PEPPY CLAM SHELLS
(Clams Casino)

1/2 cup finely chopped onion
1/2 cup finely chopped celery
1/4 cup finely chopped
  green pepper
4 Tbsp. margarine
2 Tbsp. flour
1 Tbsp. parmesan cheese

1/4 tsp. salt
Dash pepper
Dash Worcestershire sauce
1 1/2 cups cracker crumbs
1 7 1/2 oz. can minced
  clams
1 Tbsp. melted margarine

Sauté onion, celery and green pepper in margarine until tender. Stir in flour, cheese and seasonings. Add 1/4 cup cracker crumbs. Stir in undrained clams. Cook until thick. Spread in clam shells. Combine remaining crumbs with melted margarine. Sprinkle on top of mixture.
Bake at 325° for 15 minutes. Makes about 6 clam shells, depending on size of shells. Double recipe as needed.

Gloria Wittlinger

SEAFOOD STUFFED MUSHROOMS

15-20 med. mushrooms
8 Tbsp. melted margarine
1 7 1/2oz. can crabmeat
2 eggs, lightly beaten

6 Tbsp. soft bread crumbs
2 Tbsp. mayonnaise
2 Tbsp. chives or onion
1 tsp. lemon juice

Remove stems from mushrooms and chop fine. Brush mushroom caps with seven tbsp. margarine. Arrange on lightly greased baking pan. In a small bowl combine eggs, crabmeat, four Tbsp. bread crumbs, mayonnaise, chives and juice. Fill caps. Combine two tbps. bread crumbs and one tbsp. margarine. Sprinkle over caps.
Bake at 375° for 15 minutes.

Estelle Dunlap

(31)

VEGGIE SQUARES

2 lg. cans Pillsbury crescent rolls
2 8oz. pkgs. cream cheese, softened
1 cup mayonnaise
1 pkg. original ranch dressing mix
Assorted veggies, chopped fine

Spread crescent roll dough on a large cookie sheet or jelly roll pan. Bake at 375° for 8-10 minutes. Cool.
Mix cream cheese, mayonnaise and dressing mix together until smooth. Spread on cooled dough. Top with veggie combinations.
Some suggestions: green & red bell pepper; small onion or small bunch of green onions with tops; carrots, broccoli, cauliflower, zucchini, or yellow squash. Let stand in refrigerator overnight. Cut and serve.
NOTE: This can also be used for a dish to pass supper or for picnics or reunions.

Joan Pearson

MINIATURE HAM BALLS

1 1/2 lbs. ground meat (half ham, half pork - meat market will do this for you)
3/4 cup milk
3/4 cup bread crumbs
2 eggs (or eggbeaters)
1/4 tsp. pepper

Mix together and make into 30 small meatballs. Put into baking pan and pour maple syrup about half way up the side of the pan. Bake at 350° for 45 minutes.
Serve on a warming tray with toothpicks.
NOTE: This also works for a brunch. They may be made a week ahead and frozen.

Christa Caldwell

CHEESE BALL

2 8 oz. pkgs. cream cheese, softened
1 small jar green olives with pimentos
1 small can pitted black olives
Several dashes Worcestershire & Tabasco sauce

Drain olives and chop fine. Add to the cream cheese and sauces. Mix well. Using gloves or plastic wrap, shape into a ball or balls. Roll in chopped nuts if desired. Chill overnight.

Joan Pearson

FAUX CHAMPAGNE

For each 4 oz. champagne glass:
2 oz. apple juice
2 oz. ginger ale

Wonderful for times when you want it to look like champagne but be non-alcoholic!

Christa Caldwell

LETHAL LEMONADE

1 lg. can frozen orange juice
1 lg. can frozen lemonade (12 oz.)
Water as directed on cans
2 cups tea (use 4 tea bags)
1 1/2 cups sugar
2 1/2 cups whiskey

Mix well and freeze. At serving time, fill glass 2/3 full with the frozen mixture. Add 7-up or a lemon-lime drink.

Christa Caldwell

LOW-FAT EGGNOG

4 cups skim milk, more may be needed
1 12oz. can evaporated skim milk
1 8 oz. carton frozen egg product, thawed
1/2 cup sugar
1/2 cup light rum
1 tsp. vanilla

Over medium heat stir both milks, egg and sugar about 10 minutes or until slightly thickened. Do not boil. Stir over a bowl of ice water and add rum and vanilla. Stir in more skim milk until desired thickness is reached. Sprinkle with nutmeg. Serves 12.

Virginia Strablow

HOT CIDER

2 gallons apple cider
1 cup brown sugar
6 cinnamon sticks
1 Tbsp. cloves
1 Tbsp. allspice
1 orange, cut in half
2 apples, cut in half

Mix all together and heat in a large kettle for one hour.
NOTE: Served at the Col Wm. Bond House in years past.

Alma Miller

PUNCH

3 6 oz. cans frozen tangerine juice
1 6 oz. can frozen pineapple juice
1 6 oz. can frozen orange juice
2 32 oz. bottles lemon-lime soda

Add water to concentrated juices as directed. Mix in bowl
and add soda. Serve with an ice ring.

Alma Miller

PUNCH

3 bottles ginger ale
1 pkg. raspberry jello
1 pkg. frozen raspberries
1 6 oz. can frozen pink lemonade
1 bottle of alcohol of choice

Dissolve jello in one cup boiling ginger ale. Mix all
ingredients together. Also good without the alcohol.

Virginia Strablow

(35)

QUICK PUNCH

1 12oz. can frozen lemonade
1 12oz. can frozen orange juice
1 12oz. can pineapple juice
2 lg. bottles ginger ale

Thaw juices and mix with ginger ale.

Virginia Strablow

TEA PUNCH

4 cups very strong tea
1 bottle maraschino cherries
1 can pineapple tidbits

Let chill overnight then add two to three large bottles of ginger ale before serving.

Virginia Strablow

RECIPES & NOTES

RECIPES & NOTES

BREADS

BAKING POWDER BISCUITS

2 cups flour
3 tsp. baking powder
1/2 tsp. salt
1/3 cup shortening
3/4 cup milk

Sift dry ingredients in bowl. Cut in shortening until mixture resembles course crumbs. Make a well and add milk all at once. Stir quickly with fork until dough follows fork around the bowl. Turn onto a lightly floured surface (dough should be soft). knead gently 10 to 12 strokes. Roll or pat dough 1/2 inch thick. Dip 2 1/2 inch biscuit cutter in flour. Cut dough straight down. Bake on ungreased cookie sheet at 350° for 15 to 18 minutes.

Laura Shortridge

GRANDMA'S BAKING POWDER BISCUITS

2 cups sifted flour
1/3 tsp. baking soda
1/2 tsp. salt
1 Tbsp. baking powder (level)
1/3 cup Crisco
1 cup buttermilk (room temperature)

Sift first four ingredients together twice. Cut in Crisco and slowly add buttermilk. Mix well. Roll out and cut with a cookie cutter. Bake on a well greased pan with sides touching at 375° to 400° for 10 to 12 minutes. Don't overtake.
Yield: 9 large biscuits. Good as biscuits, shortcake or chicken fricassee.

Gerry Reynolds

OLD FASHIONED BISCUITS OR SHORTCAKE

2 cups flour
3 tsp. baking powder
1/2 tsp. salt
2 Tbsp. sugar (omit for biscuits)
1/3 cup shortening
2 eggs
Milk

Sift flour, baking powder and salt. Add sugar. Beat the eggs in a separate cup. Add enough milk to the eggs to make one cup. Add to dry ingredients with shortening.
Bake at 450° for 8 to 10 minutes or until lightly browned. These never fail.

Betty Roadarmel

APPLE KUCHEN

2 cups flour
2/3 cup milk
5 Tbsp. shortening
3 tsp. baking powder

1 tsp. salt
2 Tbsp. sugar
1 egg
4 to 5 apples

Mix egg and milk and add dry ingredients with shortening. Spread in a greased cookie tin. Peel and slice apples and place on dough. Mix 3/4 cup sugar and 1/2 tsp. cinnamon. Sprinkle on top of the apple dough and dot with butter.
Bake at 400° for 20 to 25 minutes.

Inez Metz

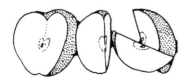

(38)

MELLOW APPLE LOAF

1/2 cup soft shortening
2/3 cup brown sugar
2 eggs
2 cups flour, sifted
1 cup applesauce

1 tsp. baking powder
1 tsp. baking soda
1/2 tsp. salt
1/2 cup chopped nuts

Mix together shortening, sugar and eggs. Stir in applesauce. Sift together flour, baking powder, soda and salt. Mix all together and add nuts.
Bake at 350° for 50 to 55 minutes.

Arvilla Hall

ALOHA LOAF

2 cups margarine or butter
4 cups sugar
8 eggs
2 cups ripe bananas,mashed
8 cups flour, sifted
2 cups shredded coconut

4 tsp. baking powder
2 tsp. baking soda
1 1/2 tsp. salt
2 15oz.cans crushed
    pineapple

Cream margarine and sugar until light and fluffy. Add eggs and mix well. Stir in banana. Sift together flour, baking powder, baking soda and salt. Add to creamed mixture and mix well. Fold in undrained pineapple and coconut. pour in four greased and floured 9"x5" loaf pans.
Bake at 350° for one hour and 10 minutes. Remove from pans and cool.

Virginia Strablow

EGGNOG BREAD

1/4 cup melted butter
3/4 cup sugar
2 eggs, beaten
2 1/4 cups flour
2 tsp. baking powder
1 tsp. salt

1 cup eggnog
1/2 cup chopped pecans
1/2 cup raisins
1/2 cup chopped red &
  green candied cherries

In a large bowl, combine butter, sugar and eggs and mix well. Combine the flour, baking powder and salt. Stir into butter mixture alternately with eggnog; mix only until dry ingredients are moistened. Fold in pecans, raisins and cherries. Spoon into a greased loaf pan.
Bake at 350° for one hour or until bread tests done. Cool before slicing.

Patricia O. Few

BLUEBERRY COFFEECAKE

Cake:
2 cups flour
1 cup sugar
1 Tbsp. baking powder
1/4 tsp. salt

1 1/2 cups blueberries
2 eggs
1/4 cup melted butter
3/4 to 1 cup milk

Topping:
1/2 cup flour
3/4 cup sugar

1/2 tsp. cinnamon
1/3 cup butter, softened

Cake: Mix together the first four ingredients. Add the blueberries. Make a well in the center and add eggs, butter and milk. Mix quickly with spoon until batter forms. Put batter into a greased 9" by 12" baking pan. Mix the topping ingredients together and cover the batter with the crumbs.
Bake at 350° for 30 to 35 minutes or until done.

Good neighbor,
Dave Marmon

CREAM CHEESE COFFEECAKE

1 stick margarine
8 oz. cream cheese
1 ¼ cups sugar
2 eggs
¼ cup milk

1 tsp. vanilla
2 cups flour
1 tsp. baking powder
½ tsp. baking soda
¼ tsp. salt

Cream margarine, cream cheese and sugar together. Add eggs and beat well. Add dry ingredients alternately with the milk. Mix well. Pour into 9" by 13" greased pan. Mix together 1 cup brown sugar, 1 tsp. cinnamon, 1 cup flour and 1 stick of margarine. Put this mixture over top of batter.
Bake at 350° for 35 to 40 minutes.

Virginia Strablow

STICKY ROLLS

2 Rich's bread dough
1 box vanilla pudding, not
   instant
1 stick margarine
1 cup brown sugar

Nuts & raisins

1 Tbsp. Vanilla
1/3 cup milk

Grease a 9" by 13" pan. Break each bread dough loaf into 24 pieces (48 altogether) and form into balls. Place the balls into the bottom of the pan.
Melt margarine. Turn off heat and add pudding, brown sugar, cinnamon and mix. Stir in milk. Spoon mixture on top of the dough. Let rise to the top of the pan (3 to 5 hours).
Bake at 350° 20 to 25 minutes. Cool 5 to 10 minutes and invert.

Virginia Strablow

CAROLYN'S STICKY BUNS

1 stick margarine
2 cans crescent rolls
½ cup chopped nuts
1 cup brown sugar

Melt margarine. Put 2 Tbsp. in bottom of 10" round pan. Sprinkle 3 Tbsp. chopped nuts over this. Boil together for one minute the remaining margarine, nuts, brown sugar and 2 Tbsp. water. Cut each tube of crescent rolls into eight pieces. Separate each a little and place in pan. They will be crowded. Pour hot sauce over.
Bake at 350° for about 25 minutes. Cool three minutes. Turn upside down onto a serving plate.

Christa Caldwell

FASTNACT KUECHELES

4 cups flour
2 eggs
1 small yeast cake
¼ cup margarine, melted
1 scant tsp. salt
¼ cup sugar
1 ¾ cup milk, scalded and cooled

Put flour into a bowl and make a well in the center. Soften yeast in ½ cup warm milk with ½ Tbsp. sugar. Pour into well. Let rise until foamy and light. Add remaining ingredients. Work into a dough and knead. Cover and let rise until very light, about an hour. Turn onto floured board and roll ½" thick. Cut and let stand until light.
Fry in oil at 375° raised side down until brown. Turn and brown the other side about one minute.

Estelle Dunlap

GRANDMA'S BUCKWHEAT PANCAKES

1 cup buttermilk
¾ cup buckwheat flour
1/8 cup all purpose flour
1 egg, beaten well
½ tsp. salt
1 scant tsp. baking soda in ¼ cup buttermilk

The night before mix buttermilk and flours. Do not refrigerate. In the morning add the egg and soda in buttermilk and mix.

Cook at 375° in an electric fry pan or on top of the stove on a griddle that is hot enough to bubble water when sprinkled on it. Makes 8 pancakes.
Note: These pancakes will be thinner than other pancakes. To make 16 to 18 pancakes, double ingredients except for the egg.

Gerry Reynolds

NEW ENGLAND DOUGHNUTS

¼ cup shortening
1 cup sugar
½ tsp. salt
2 eggs
1 cup mashed potatoes

4 cups flour
3 tsp. baking powder
½ tsp. nutmeg
½ tsp. baking soda
1 cup sour or buttermilk

Blend shortening, sugar, salt and eggs. Stir in freshly cooked mashed potatoes. Sift flour with baking powder, nutmeg and baking soda. Add alternately with milk. Roll out to ½" thickness. Cut with doughnut cutter and fry in hot shortening heated to 375°

Alma Miller

MEXICAN CORN BREAD

2 12oz. pkgs. corn bread mix
1 cup milk
3 eggs
#1 can creamed corn
cheese

2 lbs. ground beef
2 green peppers, sliced
2 onions, sliced
1   cup   grated   cheddar

Combine ground beef, peppers and onions and brown. Mix together corn bread mix, milk, eggs and creamed corn. Pour half of this mixture into a greased 9"x13" pan. Cover with the ground beef mixture. Sprinkle cheese over that. Add remainder of corn bread mixture.

Bake at 450° for 25 to 30 minutes. Very easy to reheat or serve cold. Satisfies big appetites on small budgets.

SHREDDED WHEAT BREAD
Break 6 shredded wheat biscuits into a bowl. Add 2 cups boiling water and let stand until cool. Add 2 cups scalded milk and 2 Tbsp. shortening, 1/2 cup molasses and 1 Tbsp. salt. Stir to mix well. When lukewarm add 1 yeast cake dissolved in 1/4 cup warm water. Add 5 cups white flour, one at a time, stirring with a knife until well mixed. Finish like white bread.

Betsy Diachun

TENNESSEE CORN BREAD

1 cup flour, sifted
1 cup yellow cornmeal
4 tsp. baking powder
2 Tbsp. sugar

Dash of salt
1 cup milk
1/4 cup shortening
1 egg

Preheat oven to 425°. Grease corn bread pan. Blend all ingredients and beat by hand one minute. Pour into pan and bake for 20 minutes. Test bread to be sure it is done.

Esther Casselman

AMISH FRIENDSHIP BREAD

BREAD STARTER

In a non-metal bowl, mix:

2 cups flour
2 Tbsp. sugar
1 tsp. salt
1 pkg. active dry yeast

Add 2 cups warm water (105-115°). Stir until well mixed using a non-metal spoon. Cover loosely with plastic wrap and let stand three days, stirring once each day. The mixture will be bubbly and have a sour cream aroma. This is the mixture that you give away to your friends that is used to begin the friendship bread process. It may be stored in the refrigerator for up to 14 days.

HOW THE FRIENDSHIP GROWS
&
HOW TO MAKE THE BREAD

REMINDERS: Do NOT use metal bowls or spoons for mixing; Do NOT refrigerate from this point on; Make sure bowl is tightly covered; It is normal for batter to thicken, bubble and ferment!

Begin with one cup of starter from your friend or your own

DAY 1: Do nothing
DAY 2: Stir and re-cover bowl
DAY 3: Stir and re-cover bowl
DAY 4: Stir and re-cover bowl
DAY 5: Stir and re-cover bowl
DAY 6: Add 1 cup flour, 1 cup sugar, 1 cup milk, stir and recover bowl.
DAY 7: Stir and re-cover bowl
DAY 8: Stir and re-cover bowl
DAY 9: Stir and re-cover bowl
DAY 10: In a large bowl, combine batter, 1 cup flour, 1 cup sugar and 1 cup of milk. Mix well. Pour four 1 cup starters into small plastic containers and seal. Keep one for yourself and give the rest away!!!

(con't)

AMISH FRIENDSHIP BREAD (CON'T)

To the remaining batter (which will be several tablespoons) add the following:

1 cup oil	2 cups flour
1 cup sugar	1/2 cup milk
1 tsp. vanilla	1/2 tsp. baking soda
3 large eggs	1 box instant vanilla
1 1/2 tsp. baking powder	pudding
2 tsp. cinnamon	Extra cinnamon & sugar

Pour into two large, well greased and sugared (cinnamon and sugar mixed) loaf pans. Sprinkle cinnamon and sugar on top.

Bake at 325° for one hour. Cake pans may be used. Test after 1/2 hour with toothpick for doneness.

Our volunteers at NCHS can attest to how good this bread tastes...Melissa & Rosemary offer it all winter long!

Rosemary Dever
Melissa Dunlap

CEREAL ZUCCHINI BREAD

1 1/4 cups wheat germ or all bran cereal	2 eggs
	1 3/4 cups sugar
3 cups flour	2 tsp. vanilla
3 tsp. baking powder	2/3 cup oil
1 tsp. salt	3 cups zucchini, grated
2 tsps. cinnamon	1 cup chopped nuts

Mix cereal, flour, baking powder, salt, cinnamon and nuts. Beat eggs. Add vanilla, sugar and oil, beating well. Stir in zucchini. Gradually add flour mixture.

Bake at 350° for one hour in two greased pans or 325° in glass pans. Cook 5-10 minutes before removing.

Inez Metz

CHOCOLATE ZUCCHINI BREAD

3 eggs, beaten
1 1/2 cups sugar
3 tsp. vanilla
1 cup oil
2 cups grated zucchini
3 cups flour
1 tsp. salt

1/2 tsp. baking powder
3 tsp. cinnamon
1 pkg.ins.choc.pudding
1/2 cup coconut
1/2 cup nuts
1/2 cup chocolate chips
1 tsp. soda

Beat eggs until light. Add sugar, vanilla and oil. Mix well. Stir in zucchini. Sift flour, salt, soda, baking powder and cinnamon. Blend with creamed mixture. Fold in coconut, dry pudding mix, nuts and chocolate chips. Put in two 9"x5" loaf pans.
Bake at 350° for one hour. When cool you may sprinkle with powdered sugar.

Virginia Strablow

PINEAPPLE ZUCCHINI BREAD

3 eggs
2 cups sugar
1cup oil
2 cups grated zucchini, packed
1/2 tsp. vanilla
3 1/2 cups flour
1/2 tsp. salt

2 tsp. baking soda
1/4 tsp. baking powder
1/2 tsp. cinnamon
1/2 tsp. nutmeg
1 lg. can crushed
    pineapple, drained *
1 cup chopped nuts

Mix together. Bake in two greased loaf pans at 350° for about 50 to 60 minutes.
* 2 cups raisins may be substituted for the pineapple.

Virginia Strablow

HERB ROLLS

1/4 cup margarine
1 1/2 tsp. parsley flakes
1/2 tsp. dill seed
1/4 tsp. onion flakes
1 pkg. refrigerator buttermilk biscuits, cut in half

Melt margarine in a 9" pie pan. Add herbs and mix well.
Roll biscuit pieces in mixture and arrange touching in pan.
Bake at 425° for 12 minutes or until brown.

Jan Robarr

PARKERHOUSE ROLLS

3 Tbsp. butter
1 tsp. salt
1/2 cup lukewarm water
6 cups sifted flour

1 pint milk
1 Tbsp. sugar
1 cake yeast

Scald milk and pour over sugar, salt and butter. Allow it to
cool. When lukewarm add yeast which has been dissolved
in the water, then add 3 cups flour. Beat hard, cover and
let rise until a frothy mass. Add the remaining flour. Let
rise again until double in bulk, then place on board and
knead lightly. Pull to 1/2" thickness. Use biscuit cutter
and cut out rolls. Brush each one with butter, fold over and
press edge down. Place in greased pan and let rise until
very light.
Bake at 425° for 15 minutes. Makes three dozen.

Estelle Dunlap

RECIPES & NOTES

RECIPES & NOTES

CAKES, COOKIES

&

CANDY

APPLE CAKE

1 1/2 cups cooking oil	3 cups flour
2 cups sugar	1 tsp. salt
3 eggs, beaten	1 tsp. baking soda
4 apples, peeled & chopped	2 tsps. vanilla

Mix first 3 ingredients together and beat with mixer. Add apples and stir. Sift flour, soda and salt together and add to other ingredients. Mix by hand then add vanilla.

Bake at 325° in 2 greased 9" layer pans for 40 minutes.

Frost with:

1/2 cup butter	1/2 cup evaporated milk
1 cup brown sugar	1 tsp. vanilla

Melt butter with brown sugar. Add milk and boil for five minutes. Let cool. Add vanilla, mix well and frost cake.

Maggie Lupo

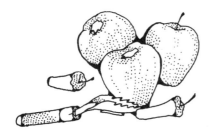

BALL CAKE

One cup butter, two of sugar. Stir butter and sugar together then add 1 egg and 1 cup flour. Stir well and add 1 egg and 1 cup flour and stir well, then the last cup of flour mixed with 1 tsp. cream of tartar. Stir in one last egg then 1 cup milk with 1/2 tsp. baking soda. Summary: 4 eggs, 4 cups flour, 1 cup milk, 1/2 tsp. soda, 2 cups sugar, 1 tsp. cream of tartar.

Bake in a heat proof bowl in moderate oven until done! When cool frost curved side up. c.1832

BUNDT CAKE

1 pkg. yellow cake mix
1 tsp. butter flavoring
1 pkg. inst. vanilla pudding
3/4 cup oil

3/4 cup water
4 eggs
1 tsp. vanilla

Combine the first five ingredients. Beat in the eggs, one at a time. Add vanilla.

Filling: Mix
1/2 to 3/4 cup nuts
1/4 cup sugar
2 tsp. cinnamon

Grease bundt pan well. Pour half of the batter, then the filling, then the rest of the batter.
Bake at 350° for 45 minutes.

Icing:
1 cup powdered sugar
1 1/2 Tbsp. milk
1/2 tsp. butter flavoring
1 tsp. vanilla

Mix and drizzle over cake after removing from pan.

Eileen Dever

ROMEO & JULIET CAKE
Juliet: 1 cup white sugar; 6 egg whites, well beaten; 1 Tbsp. butter; 1 1/2 cups flour; 1 heaping tsp. baking powder, 4 Tbsp. milk.
Romeo: 1 cup sugar; 1 Tbsp. butter; 6 egg yolks; 1 cup flour; 4 Tbsp. milk; 1 heaping tsp. baking powder.
Bake is separate tins.
Frosting: Beat 2 egg whites until stiff. Add rind and juice of 1 lemon. Add a little sugar. Beat until stiff.

CARROT CAKE

2 cups flour
1 tsp. baking powder
2 tsp. baking soda
1 tsp. salt
2 tsp. cinnamon
1 3/4 cups sugar
1 8 oz. can crushed
   pineapple

1 cup vegetable oil]
1 tsp. vanilla
2 cups carrots, shredded
1 cup coconut, flaked
1 cup nuts, chopped (opt)
3 eggs
Raisins (opt)

Drain pineapple and save the liquid for the frosting. Raisins may be added to the batter (about one cup) instead of the nuts or in addition to.

Mix dry ingredients in a bowl. Make a well in the center and add in order: sugar, oil, eggs and vanilla. Beat with a wooden spoon until smooth. Stir in carrots, coconut, nuts, pineapple and mix until well blended. Pour into a greased and lightly floured oblong cake pan (9x13).

Bake at 350° for 45 minutes or until done. DO NOT UNDERBAKE! This is a very moist cake. Frost with cream cheese frosting.

Joan Pearson

CREAM CHEESE FROSTING

1 3 oz. pkg. cream cheese, softened
1/4 cup margarine, softened
2 cups confectioners sugar
1/2 tsp. vanilla
2 tsp. milk or pineapple juice

Beat the cream cheese and margarine and beat in the sugar and vanilla. Add milk or juice until spreading consistency. Sprinkle top with shredded coconut if desired.

Joan Pearson

CHEESE CAKE

Cake:

5 8 oz. pkgs. cream cheese
1 1/2 cups graham cracker
  crumbs
1 1/4 cup sugar
2 Tbsp. flour

2 tsp. vanilla
2 Tbsp. lemon juice
2/3 cup butter
1 tsp. cinnamon
6 large eggs

Topping:

1 pt. sour cream
1/4 cup sugar

1 tsp. vanilla
1 can cherry pie filling

Beat cream cheese, two eggs, 1/2 cup sugar and flour. In another bowl, beat four eggs and 1/2 cup sugar until fluffy. Add vanilla and lemon juice and fold into cream cheese mixture.

Line a spring form pan with a mixture of cracker crumbs, the butter, cinnamon and 1/4 cup sugar. Pour cream cheese mixture into it.

Bake at 375° for 50 minutes or until set.

Mix sour cream, sugar and vanilla. Remove cake from oven and spread mixture over the top. Return to the oven and bake for 10 more minutes.

Remove from the oven and let cool. Cover cake with cherry pie filling and serve.

Alma Miller

JENNIE'S FRUIT CAKE

Mix together 2 cups sugar, 1 cup butter, 1 cup sour milk, 3 eggs, 2 1/2 cups flour, 1 cup raisins, 2 tsp. cinnamon, 1 tsp. cloves, 2 tsp. baking soda, 1/2 tsp. nutmeg.
Bake in a medium oven for 45 minutes.

LIGHT & LUSCIOUS
STRAWBERRY CHEESECAKE

1 1/2 cups graham cracker
  crumbs
3 Tbsp. melted butter
1 15 oz.pkg. ricotta cheese,
hulled
  part skim
2/3 cup flour
4 eggs, separated
2 Tbsp. lemon peel, grated

2 tsp. vanilla
1 cup sugar, divided
1 cup non-fat sour cream
3   pints   strawberries,

  and divided
4 tsp. lemon juice
1/4 cup currant jelly,
  melted

Preheat oven to 300°. In a medium bowl, combine crumbs and butter. Press mixture onto bottom and two inches up the side of a lightly greased, nine inch spring form pan and set aside.

In a large bowl, beat ricotta cheese until smooth. Add flour, egg yolks, lemon peel, vanilla and 3/4 cup of the sugar and mix well. Stir in sour cream and blend thoroughly.

In a medium bowl, beat egg whites until stiff but not dry. Fold into cheese mixture. Pour into prepared crust and smooth the top. Bake one hour. Turn off oven. Cool in oven one hour with door ajar. Remove from oven and chill thoroughly.

Puree two pints of strawberries with the remaining 1/4 cup sugar and the lemon juice. Strain sauce to remove seeds. Cover and chill. To serve: halve the remaining strawberries and arrange on top of the cake. Brush strawberries with the melted jelly. Cut cake into wedges and serve with the sauce.

Good Neighbor,
Dave Marmon

SILVER CAKE (GOOD)
Beat 1/2 cup butter to a cream. Add 1 1/2 cups sugar and beat. Add 1 cup cold water and 2 1/2 cups flour and beat hard for 5 minutes. Then stir in 2 tsp. baking powder, then the well beaten whites of 4 eggs, 1/2 tsp. salt and 1 tsp. vanilla or other flavoring. Bake carefully!

CHOCOLATE CAKE

2 cups flour	1 cup boiling water
2 cups sugar	2 eggs
1/2 cup cocoa	2 tsps. vanilla
1 1/2 tsp. salt	1 cup buttermilk, room
1/2 cup shortening	temp.
	1 tsp. soda

Sift first four ingredients. Add shortening and cream mixture. Add boiling water and mix well. Add eggs and vanilla and mix well. Add room temperature buttermilk with soda dissolved in it. Mix well and put in layer pans, or a loaf pan or 9x13 pan greased and lightly floured. Batter will be thin.
Bake at 350° for 30 to 35 minutes.

Frosting:

1/4 cup butter, melted	2 cups powdered sugar
1/4 cup cocoa	1+ Tbsp. milk
1 1/2 tsp. vanilla	

Mix and spread on cake.

Gerry Reynolds

MOIST CHOCOLATE CAKE

1 cup sugar	1 cup sour milk
1/4 cup butter or margarine	with 1 tsp. soda dissolved
2 Tbsp. cocoa	1 1/2 cups flour
Pinch of salt	1 egg

Cream sugar and butter. Add milk and mix. Stir in dry ingredients and add the egg last.
Pour into 9 inch pan that has been greased and floured.
Bake at 350° for 25 minutes.
A good way to use milk that sours. Freezes well.

Virginia Strablow

(54)

MIN'S CHOCOLATE CAKE

2 cups flour	2 eggs
2 cups sugar	2 tsps. vanilla
1/2 cup cocoa	1 cup buttermilk, room
1/2 cup shortening	temp.
1 1/2 tsp. salt	with 1 tsp. baking soda

Sift dry ingredients and put in mixer. Cream with shortening. Add eggs and vanilla and mix well. Add buttermilk and baking soda. Batter will be thin. Put in layer pans or 9"x13" pan.
Bake at 350° for 30 to 35 minutes.

FROSTING: Boiled or chocolate (My favorite is Choco-bake)
1/4 cup butter, melted
1 envelope Choco-bake or 3 Tbsp. cocoa & 1 Tbsp. oil
1 1/2 tsp. vanilla
2 cups confectioners sugar
1 - 2 Tbsp. milk or more for right consistency

Beat all ingredients together until smooth. Spread on cooled cake.

Gerry Reynolds

CHOCOLATE SUNDAE CAKE

Make your favorite moist chocolate cake in a 9"x13" pan. While the cake is still warm poke holes 1/2" apart all over the cake.
Pour one can of sweetened condensed milk evenly over the cake. Then spread one jar of Mrs. Richardson's caramel fudge topping over the milk. Refrigerate until cool.
Spread on a layer of whipped cream. Crush six Skor or Heath bars into crumbs and sprinkle over the whipped cream. M-m-m-m!

Pat O. Few

(55)

CRAZY CAKE

3 cups flour, sifted
2 cups sugar
6 Tbsp. Hershey's cocoa
2 tsp. soda
1 tsp. salt

3/4 cup melted shortening
  or margarine
2 Tbsp. vinegar
2 tsp. vanilla
2 cups cold water

Mix all dry ingredients in a bowl. Sift them into an ungreased 9"x13" pan. With the back of a wooden spoon, make three holes in the dry ingredients. Pour melted shortening in one, vinegar in the second and vanilla in the third. Pour water over the top. Mix and blend thoroughly until batter is smooth.

Bake at 350° for 50 to 60 minutes or until done.

Frost as desired. Kids love this cake!

Joan Pearson

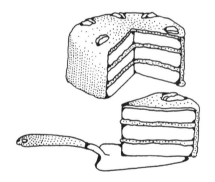

SOLID CHOCOLATE CAKE

Mix 1 1/2 cups sugar, 1/2 cup butter, 1/2 cup sour milk, 1/2 cup cold water, 1 whole egg and 2 egg yolks. Then add 2 squares chocolate, melted, 1/2 tsp. baking soda, 1 tsp. baking powder and 2 cups flour. Mix and bake.

CHOCOLATE FROSTING

Stir together 1 1/2 cups confectioners sugar, 6 tsp. cocoa, butter the size of an egg with a little hot coffee. Beat with a fork until right to spread.

OLD SOUTH FRUITCAKE

5 cups sifted all purpose flour
1/2 tsp. baking soda
1 tsp. cinnamon
1/2 tsp. allspice
3 eggs, well beaten
1 cup melted butter (1/2 lb)
1 cup orange marmalade
1 cup nuts, coarsely chopped
1/2 cup candied lemon peel,
   finely chopped
1 cup currents (1/2 box)
Corn syrup

2 tsp. baking powder
1 tsp. salt
1 tsp. nutmeg
1/2 tsp. cloves
1 1/2 cups light molasses,
   (12 oz.jar)
1 1/2 cups applesauce
1 cup candied orange peel,
   finely chopped
3 cups golden seedless
   raisins (1 box)

Sift together dry ingredients. Beat eggs and blend in molasses, butter, marmalade and applesauce. Dredge combined nuts, peels, raisins and currants with one cup dry ingredients. Blend remaining dry ingredients into molasses mixture. Stir in fruit and nut mixture. Pour into greased, wax paper lined 10" tube pan.

Bake at 250° for 3 hours. Remove from pan and cool. Peel off wax paper. Glaze with hot corn syrup and decorate.

Inez Metz

LEMON PUDDING CAKE

1/4 cup butter or margarine
1 1/2 cups sugar
4 egg yolks
1/4 cup flour, unsifted

2 cups milk
1 tsp. grated lemon peel
1/2 cup lemon juice
4 egg whites

Beat butter and sugar until well blended. Beat in yolks. Blend in flour and milk. Stir in lemon peel and juice. Beat egg whites until soft peaks form and fold into lemon mixture. Put into a casserole (1 1/2 qt.size). Set casserole in a container with one inch of boiling water.

Bake at 350° 45 minutes or until golden brown or when knife inserted is clean. Let cool before serving.

Ruth Jerge

LAZY DAISY OATMEAL CAKE

1 1/4 cups boiling water
1 cup oatmeal
1/2 cup butter or margarine
1 cup white sugar
1 cup brown sugar, packed
1 tsp. vanilla

1 1/2 cups flour
1 tsp. baking soda
1/2 tsp. salt
3/4 tsp. cinnamon
1/4 tsp. nutmeg
2 eggs

Pour boiling water over oats and let stand 20 minutes. Beat butter. Add sugars and beat until fluffy. Add vanilla and eggs. Add oatmeal mixture and mix well. Add flour, soda, salt, cinnamon and nutmeg. Pour into a 9" square pan.

Bake at 350° 50 to 55 minutes. Frost with Lazy Daisy Frosting:

1 1/4 cup butter or margarine
1/2 cup brown sugar, packed
3 Tbsp. half & half (or milk)

1/3 cup chopped nuts
3/4 cup coconut

Combine all ingredients and spread over cake. Broil until bubbly. Cake can be served warm or cold.

Virginia Strablow

PINEAPPLE NUT CAKE

2 cups flour
2 cups crushed pineapple,
   drained
2 cups sugar

2 tsp. baking soda
2 eggs
1 cup walnuts

Grease and flour a 9"x13" pan. Stir all ingredients together and pour into pan.

Bake about 40 minutes at 350°. Frost cake:
8 oz.pkg. cream cheese
1/2 cup butter

1 Tbsp. vanilla
1 1/2 to 2 cups powdered
   sugar

Whip cream cheese and butter. Add vanilla and enough sugar to make icing spreadable. Frost cake.

Arvilla Hall

CRANBERRY POUND CAKE

1 17oz. yellow cake mix	1 cup chopped cranberries
1 8oz. carton sour cream	1/2 cup chopped nuts
4 eggs	Creamy glaze

Combine dry cake mix, sour cream and eggs in a large mixing bowl. Blend at low speed until moistened. Beat two minutes at medium speed, scraping sides and bottom of bowl occasionally. Fold in cranberries and nuts. Pour batter into a generously greased and lightly floured three quart bundt pan or a 10" tube pan.

Bake at 350° for 35-45 minutes until toothpick inserted in center comes out clean. Cool for 15 minutes in pan. Remove from pan and cool completely.

CREAMY GLAZE

Melt 1/2 cup butter or margarine. Blend in 2 cups confectioners sugar and 1 1/2 tsp. vanilla. Stir in two to four Tbsps. of hot water, one Tbsp. at a time until consistency is right for spreading. I usually make the glaze very thin. Spread on top of the cake and let it drip down sides. Cake may also be dusted with confectioners sugar instead of glazing, if desired.

A great holiday cake. Keeps well!

Joan Pearson

POUND CAKE
1 pound flour, 1 pound sugar, 1 pound butter, 8 eggs, 1 tsp. rose water and 1/2 tsp. nutmeg, grated.
Mix and bake.

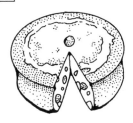

MARBLE POUND CAKE

3 cups flour
2 cups sugar
1 Tbsp. baking powder
1 tsp. salt
1 1/2 cups shortening

3/4 cup milk
6 large eggs
2 tsps. vanilla
1/2 cup chocolate syrup

Combine first eight ingredients in a large mixing bowl. Beat until blended, about 20 minutes. Combine one cup of batter and chocolate syrup and set aside. Divide remaining batter in half and pour one portion into a greased and floured bundt pan. Spoon half of reserved chocolate batter on top and repeat layers. Gently swirl with a knife.

Bake at 350° for one hour and cover loosely with aluminum foil after 50 minutes to prevent excess browning. Cool in pan 10 minutes and remove to wire rack.
Very pretty...needs no icing.

Kim A. Kuntz

TUBE PAN POUND CAKE

3 eggs
1 1/2 cups sugar
3 tsp. vanilla
3/4 cup butter, softened

2 1/4 cups flour
1 1/2 tsp. baking powder
1/4 tsp. salt
1/2 cup milk

At high speed, beat for five minutes, eggs, sugar, vanilla and butter. At low speed, add flour, salt and baking powder alternating with the milk. Beat just until smooth. Grease and flour a spring form tube pan.

Bake at 325° for 55 minutes. Cool in pan for five minutes. Remove cake from pan and place on rack.

(con't)

TUBE PAN POUND CAKE (CON'T)

GLAZE: Mix confectioners sugar with water and flavoring of choice until mixture is fairly thin. Spoon generously over warm cake. Cool completely before slicing.
OPTIONS: Add 1/4 cup fresh lemon juice and peel of one lemon instead of the vanilla for a lemon cake or add 1/2 unsweetened cocoa powder, leaving in the vanilla for a chocolate cake.
This cake has been used several times for the Thursday evening museum programs!

Patricia O. Few

STRAWBERRY SPARKLE CAKE

1 pkg. angel food cake mix
1 cup boiling water
1 3 oz.pkg. strawberry jello
Red food coloring

1pkg.frozen strawberries
1/2 pt. whipping cream or
 cool whip
2 Tbsp.sugar if using cream

Bake angel food cake as directed and cool thoroughly. Dissolve jello in boiling water. Add frozen strawberries, stir and break up. Place cake, wide side down on a cake plate. Cut a 1" layer from the top of cake and set aside. Cut a "tunnel" around the remaining cake, 1" from outer and inner edges and 1" from the bottom. Gently remove cut section and break into pieces. Add to jello and strawberry mix. Pour this mixture into the tunnel. Best to let it set a little and spoon it in). Place layer on top.
Frost with cool whip or sweetened whipped cream. Add food coloring to the whipped cream if desired.

Joan Pearson

WHIPPED CREAM FROSTING

1 cup milk
1 cup sugar
1/3 cup margarine
1 tsp. flavoring

5 Tbsp. flour
1/2 cup shortening
1/4 tsp. salt

Mix milk and flour and cook until thick. Cool completely. Add the rest of the ingredients and beat until fluffy and sugar is dissolved.
This makes a fluffy but not too sweet frosting that stays soft and doesn't shrink or harden.

Mary Newhard

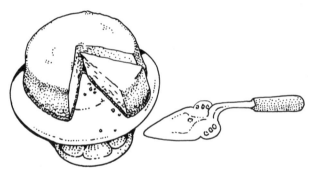

GINGERBREAD
1/2 cup melted butter, 1 egg, 1 cup brown sugar, 1 cup molasses, 1 tsp. baking soda dissolved in 1 cup warm water, 1 tsp. ginger, 1 tsp. cinnamon, 2 1/2 cups flour and 1 tsp. baking powder. When mixed put in pan and bake in medium oven for 30 to 45 minutes.

ANISE DROPS

2 eggs
3/4 cup extra fine sugar

1 cup flour
1/2 tsp. anise oil

Beat eggs and sugar together for 5 minutes in electric mixer. Add flour and beat thoroughly. Stir in anise. Drop by a demitasse spoon on greased cookie sheet (they spread). Let stand overnight.
Bake at 275° for 20 minutes. Let mellow three to four weeks. Makes five dozen.

Estelle Dunlap

KOOKIE BRITTLE

1 cup butter or margarine,
  softened
1 cup sugar
1 tsp. salt

2 cups unsifted flour
1 6 oz.pkg chocolate chips
1 cup chopped pecans
1 tsp. vanilla

In an electric mixer, cream butter or margarine and add salt and vanilla. Beat in sugar until light and fluffy scraping sides of bowl occasionally. Add flour and continue mixing until well combined. Stir in chocolate chips and nuts. Pat dough into greased 10"x15" pan.
Bake at 375° for 25 minutes or until lightly browned. Be careful not to burn around edges. When cool, break with hands into irregular pieces.

Ruth Jerge

WHITE COOKIES
1 cup sugar, 1/2 cup shortening, 1/2 cup buttermilk, 2 tsp. baking soda, 1 egg, 1/2 tsp. salt and 1 tsp. vanilla or nutmeg. Mix in enough flour to roll out.
Bake like regular cookies.

---

(63)

COLOSSAL COOKIES

1 stick margarine
1 1/2 cups white sugar
1 1/2 cups brown sugar
1 tsp. vanilla
2 1/2 tsp. baking soda
4 large eggs
1 18 oz. jar chunky peanut butter
6 cups quick oatmeal
1 12 oz. pkg. chocolate chips

Cream margarine and sugars together. Add vanilla, baking soda and eggs and mix thoroughly. Add oatmeal and mix, then chocolate chips and mix well. Drop by tsp. on ungreased cookie sheet. Press down with a fork that has been dipped in water. (You would do the same for peanut butter cookies).
Bake at 375° for eight to ten minutes. Let cool on sheet slightly. Makes five to six dozen.

Beth Strablow

GRANDMA D'S SUGAR COOKIES

2 heaping cups sugar
1 cup shortening
1 cup sour cream
1 tsp. baking soda
2 eggs
Pinch salt
6 cups flour
Nutmeg

Cream sugar and shortening. Beat in eggs and sour cream. Add dry ingredients using more or less flour as needed. Roll out and cut shapes. Place on greased cookie sheet.
Bake at 400° for eight to ten minutes.
Note: Flavoring of choice may be added.

Virginia Strablow

CHRISTMAS COOKIES

1 cup butter
2 cups sugar
3 eggs
5 cups flour
1 1/2 tsp. baking soda

1 1/2 tsp. cream of tartar
2 Tbsp. buttermilk or sour
   milk
1 tsp. vanilla

Cream butter and add sugar, a little at a time and cream. Add eggs and blend. Add vanilla, milk in which baking soda is dissolved, and flour which has been sifted with the cream of tartar. Mix well adding more flour as necessary so dough can roll easily. Roll, cut and place on greased cookie sheet.
Bake at 450° for seven minutes. Ovens vary. Try 400° for eight minutes.

Inez Metz

COWBOY COOKIES

5 sticks unsalted butter
   softened
1 2/3 cups brown sugar
1 cup granulated sugar
3 eggs, lightly beaten
2 tsp. vanilla

2 tsp. cinnamon
4 cups flour
2 tsp. baking powder
6 cups oatmeal,
   old fashioned
2 cups raisins

Preheat oven to 425°. Line several cookie sheets with baking parchment. Mix butter and sugar until smooth. Do not over mix. Add eggs, vanilla and cinnamon and combine. Add flour and baking powder and gently mix again. Fold in oatmeal and raisins. Scoop out dough with 2-oz. ice cream scoop or 1/4 cup measure, well packed. Place on cookie sheets and flatten with a wet fork.
Bake 10 minutes. Cookies will be slightly underdone. They will continue baking after being removed from the oven. Cool several minutes and transfer to a rack. Yield: Three dozen.

Betty Roadarmel

LEMON WAFERS

2 cups oats, uncooked
1 1/2 cups flour, plus extra
for your hands
1 tsp. baking powder
1/2 tsp. baking soda
1 1/4 cups sugar, plus more
for flattening cookies
1/2 cup margarine, softened

1/2 cup plain non-fat or
lemon low-fat yogurt
2 egg whites or 1 egg
1 Tbsp. grated lemon peel
1/2 tsp. vanilla
Non-stick cooking spray
1/4 cup powdered sugar

Combine the oats, flour, baking powder and baking soda in a bowl and set aside. In another bowl, beat the sugar and margarine until creamy. Add yogurt, egg whites (or egg), lemon peel and vanilla. Beat well. Gradually add dry ingredients and mix well. Cover and chill one to three hours. Preheat oven to 375°. Spray cookie sheets with non-stick spray. With lightly floured hands, shape dough into one inch balls. Place three inches apart on cookie sheets. Flatten to 1/8" thickness with bottom of glass dipped in sugar.
Bake 10 to 12 minutes or until edges are lightly browned. Cool two minutes on sheet and remove to wire rack. Sift powdered sugar over warm cookies. Cook completely. Yield: Four dozen.

Betty Roadarmel

APPLE WALNUT OATMEAL COOKIES

1 1/4 cups applesauce
3/4 cup brown sugar
1/2 cup granulated sugar
1 egg
1 tsp. vanilla
1 1/2 cups flour
1 tsp. baking soda
1 tsp. cinnamon
3 cups oats, quick or regular

1/2 tsp. salt (optional)
1/4 tsp. ground nutmeg
1/2 tsp. allspice
1/2 tsp. ground cloves
1 small red apple unpeeled
and diced
3/4 cup chopped walnuts
3/4 cup chopped raisins

(con't next page)

APPLE WALNUT OATMEAL COOKIES (CON'T)

Preheat oven to 375°.
Sift flour, salt, baking soda and spices and set aside. Beat applesauce and sugar well, then add egg and vanilla. Mix and add to the flour mixture. Mix oats with the apples, walnuts and raisins and add to the above mixture. Put on an ungreased cookie sheet with a tablespoon about 2 inches apart.
Bake eight to nine minutes for a chewy cookie or 10-11 minutes for a crispy cookie, checking with a toothpick. Cool on sheet two to three minutes, then place on wire rack. Will keep fresh one to two days at room temperature; two to four days in refrigerator. May be frozen to maintain quality, then microwave 10 to 15 seconds before serving.
OPTION: For a good, basic cookie dough leave out the underlined items.

Don Stopp

PLUMP, SOFT MOLASSES COOKIES

1/2 cup shortening
1/2 cup sugar
1 egg
1 cup dark molasses
1 Tbsp. lemon juice
3 1/2 cups sifted flour

1 tsp. cinnamon
3/4 tsp. ground cloves
1/2 tsp. ginger
2 tsp. baking soda
1/2 tsp. salt
1/3 cup boiling water

Cream shortening and sugar together. Beat in egg. Add molasses and lemon juice, blending well. Add baking soda to boiling water. Sift all other dry ingredients together and mix with shortening mixture and soda and water. Chill dough thoroughly (overnight is best). Drop by teaspoonfuls on greased cookie sheet. Sprinkle with sugar.
Bake at 350° for eight to ten minutes. Yield: 4 dozen. For larger cookies drop by tablespoonfuls.

Joan Pearson

MOLASSES COOKIES

1 cup molasses
1 cup sugar
1 egg
3/4 cup bacon fat
5 1/2 cups flour

2 tsp. baking soda
2 tsp. ginger
1/4 cup strong, brewed
   coffee

Blend sugar, molasses, bacon fat and egg. Beat in soda, ginger and four cups flour. Add more flour to make a good consistency for rolling out. Cut into shapes.
Bake at 400°. Yield: five to six dozen.

Lois Farley

RUSSIAN RAISIN TEACAKES

1 cup butter
1/4 cup powdered sugar
1 tsp. vanilla
2 cups flour

1 cup walnuts
1 cup raisins, chopped
Additional powdered sugar

Preheat oven to 350°. In a large bowl, cream butter with 1/4 cup powdered sugar and vanilla until light and fluffy. Stir in flour, walnuts and raisins. Cover and refrigerate until firm. Shape dough into one inch balls. Place on ungreased cookie sheets.
Bake for 10 minutes in upper third of the oven. Roll warm cookies in powdered sugar. Cool. Roll again in powdered sugar.

Good Neighbor,
Dave Marmon

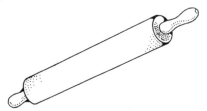

SESAME CRISPS

1 cup sesame seeds
1/2 cup shredded coconut
2 cups flour
1 tsp. baking powder
1/2 tsp. baking soda

1/2 tsp. salt
3/4 cup butter
1 cup brown sugar, packed
1 egg
1 tsp. vanilla

Toast sesame seeds and coconut in 350° oven until light brown. Cream butter and gradually add sugar and cream well. Add egg, vanilla, sesame seeds and coconut and beat well. Sift dry ingredients and mix well with wet ingredients. Shape dough into balls, using rounded tsp. of dough for each ball. Place on ungreased baking sheet and flatten to 1/8" thickness.

Bake at 350° for 10 to 12 minutes.

Arvilla Hall

PEANUT BUTTER CUP COOKIES

1 1/2 cups flour
1/3 cup baking cocoa
1 tsp. baking soda
1/4 tsp. salt
1 1/2 cups brown sugar
1 cup butter

3/4 cup peanut butter
2 eggs
2 tsp. vanilla
2 cups oats
9 oz. pkg. miniature
    peanut butter candies
(approx. 35)

Combine flour, cocoa, baking soda and salt and set aside. In a large bowl, beat sugar, butter and peanut butter until creamy. Add the eggs and vanilla and beat well. Add dry ingredients and mix well. Stir in oats and candy and mix well. Using a 1/4 cup measure, drop the cookie dough onto ungreased cookie sheets, three inches apart.

Bake at 350° for 12 to 14 minutes. Do not over bake. Cool one minute on cookie sheets and remove to wire rack. Cool completely and store tightly covered. Yield: 3 dozen.

Betty Roadarmel

EASY PEANUT BUTTER COOKIES

1 14oz. can sweetened
  condensed milk
3/4 cup peanut butter

2 cups biscuit mix
1 tsp. vanilla
Granulated sugar

In a large bowl, beat condensed milk and peanut butter until smooth. Add biscuit mix and vanilla mixing well. Shape into one inch balls and roll in sugar. Place two inches apart on ungreased baking sheet. Flatten with a fork.

Bake at 375° for six to eight minutes or until lightly browned. Do not overtake! Cool and store tightly covered at room temperature.

Virginia Strablow

WINEDROP COOKIES

1 1/4 cups packed brown sugar
1 cup shortening
1 cup medium molasses
2 eggs
1 tsp. cloves
5 cups sifted flour

2 tsp. soda dissolved in
  1 cup cold water
1 cup raisins
1 tsp.cinnamon
1 tsp. salt

Mix sugar, shortening, molasses and eggs until creamy. Sift the dry ingredients and mix with sugar mixture alternately with the soda water. Add as many raisins as desired and also chopped nuts. Put large tablespoonfuls of mixture on greased cookie sheet.

Bake at 350° for 10 to 12 minutes or until cookie is set when tested with finger. Remove from cookie sheet and let cool slightly, then dip in sifted confectioners sugar.

Ruth Jerge

BLACK BOTTOM BANANA BARS

1/2 cup butter or margarine,
  softened
1 cup sugar
1 egg
1 tsp. vanilla
1 1/2 cups mashed bananas
  (about three medium)

1 1/2 cups flour
1 tsp. baking powder
1 tsp. baking soda
1/2 tsp. salt (optional)
1/2 cup cocoa

In a mixing bowl cream butter and sugar. Add egg and vanilla and beat until thoroughly combined. Blend in bananas. Combine flour, baking powder, soda and salt and mix well. Divide batter in half and add cocoa to one half. Spread cocoa mixture in bottom of 9"x13" pan. Spoon remaining batter on top and swirl with a knife.
Bake at 350° for 40 minutes or until done.

Betty Roadarmel

RED, WHITE AND BLUEBERRY BARS

Crust:
3/4 cup flour
1/4 tsp. baking soda
1/4 tsp. salt
1/3 cup brown sugar, packed
Filling:
2 8 oz.pkgs. cream cheese,
  softened
3/4 cup sugar
2 Tbsp. flour

1 cup quick oats
1/4 cup chopped nuts
1/3 cup melted butter

1 tsp. vanilla
2 cups blueberries
1/2 cup strawberry jam
2 eggs

Crust: In a large bowl, sift together flour, baking soda and salt. Add brown sugar, oats and nuts mixing well. Add butter and mix until crumbly. Press mixture onto bottom of a lightly greased 9"x13" pan. Bake at 350° for 10 minutes.

(Con't next page)

RED, WHITE AND BLUEBERRY BARS (CON'T)

Filling:
In a large bowl, beat together cream cheese, sugar and flour until smooth. Add eggs and vanilla and beat well. Pour mixture over baked crust and spread evenly.

Bake at 350° for 25 minutes or until set. Cool completely and chill. In a small bowl, combine blueberries and jam. To serve, cut into squares and top with fruit mixture. Store in the refrigerator.

Good Neighbor,
Dave Marmon

CHARMIN' CHERRY BARS

Crust:
1 cup flour   1/4 cup confec. sugar
1/2 cup butter
Topping:
1/4 cup flour   1/2 tsp. baking powder
1/4 tsp. salt   3/4 cup sugar
2 eggs   1/2 cup maraschino
1/2 cup coconut   cherries
1/2 cup chopped walnuts

Crust:
Sift flour and sugar together and cut in butter until the mixture resembles course meal. Press mixture firmly into bottom of ungreased 9"x13" pan.

Bake at 350° for 10 minutes.
Topping:
Sift flour, baking powder, salt and sugar together then add eggs, slightly beaten. Fold in cherries, coconut and walnuts and spread over partially baked dough.

Bake 350° for 30 to 40 minutes. Cool and cut into bars.
Wonderful!

Arvilla Hall

MARSHMALLOW CHERRY BARS

3/4 cup butter or margarine
1/3 cup brown sugar, packed
1 1/2 cups sifted flour
2 env. unflavored gelatin
1/2 cup cold water
2 cups granulated sugar

1 8oz. jar maraschino
   cherries
1/2 cup cherry juice
1/2 cup chopped almonds
3 drops red food coloring
1/2 tsp. almond extract

Drain and chop cherries. Add water to juice to make 1/2 c.
Combine butter, brown sugar and flour. Mix well and press into ungreased 9"x13" pan.
Bake at 325° for 30 minutes. Set aside to cool.
Soften gelatin in 1/2 cup water. Combine white sugar and juice drained from cherries (with enough water added to make 1/2 cup). Bring to a boil over medium heat and boil two minutes. Remove from heat and stir in softened gelatin. Beat with electric mixer at medium speed until very stiff, about 20 minutes. Fold in cherries and almonds. Add food coloring and almond extract. Spread on top of baked crust in pan. let stand at room temperature until topping sets. Cut in 2" by 1" bars. Cover pan with lid or foil and leave in a cool place until time to serve. Makes about 48.

Arvilla Hall

MERINGUE SQUARES

3/4 cup margarine
1/3 cup sugar
2 egg yolks
1 1/2 cups flour

2 egg whites
1/2 cup sugar
1 cup chopped nuts
1 cup strawberry jam

Cream shortening with 1/3 cup sugar. Add egg yolks and beat well. Add sifted flour. Press mixture in ungreased 9"x13" pan.
Bake 350° for 15 minutes. Let cool. Make meringue with egg whites and 1/2 cup sugar. Fold in nuts. Spread jam on top of baked mixture and cover with the meringue.
Bake at 350° for 25 minutes.

Estelle Dunlap

WALNUT CHERRY BARS

2 1/4 cups sifted flour
1/2 cup sugar
1 cup butter
2 eggs
1 cup brown sugar, packed
1/2 tsp. salt
1/2 tsp. baking powder

1/2 tsp. vanilla
1 2oz.jar maraschino
  cherries
1/2 cup chopped walnuts
1 Tbsp. softened butter
1 cup confectioners sugar
1/2 cup flaked coconut
  (optional)

Mix flour, sugar and one cup butter until crumbly. Press into ungreased 9"x13" pan.

Bake at 350° for 20 minutes or until crust is lightly browned. Blend together eggs, brown sugar, salt, baking powder and vanilla. Drain and chop cherries, reserving liquid. Stir chopped cherries and walnuts into blended mixture. Spread on top of baked crust. Return to oven and bake 25 minutes. Remove from oven. Cool in pan on rack. Combine softened butter and confectioners sugar with enough reserved cherry liquid to spread. Spread on baked mixture and sprinkle with coconut if desired. When icing has set, cut into 2"x1" bars. Makes 48.

Arvilla Hall

OATMEAL BARS

3 cups oatmeal
1 cup butter or margarine,
  melted

1 cup brown sugar
1 cup chocolate chips
1/2 cup peanut butter

Mix oatmeal and brown sugar together. Add melted butter, mix and press into 9"x13" pan.

Bake at 400° for 10 minutes. Melt chocolate chips and peanut butter together. Spread over baked mixture and chill.

Virginia Strablow

CHIPMUNK BARS

1 cup boiling water
1/2 lb. chopped dates
1 3/4 cup flour
1/4 cup cocoa
1 tsp. baking soda
1/2 tsp. salt

1 cup margarine
1 cup sugar
2 eggs
1 tsp. vanilla
1 cup chocolate chips
1 cup chopped nuts

Pour water over dates and set aside. Cream margarine and sugar. Add eggs and vanilla. Sift flour, salt, soda and cocoa together. Add this mixture to the first mixture, then add dates. Pour into 15"x10"x1" pan, greased on bottom only. Sprinkle top with chocolate chips and nuts. Press lightly into batter.

Bake at 350° for 25 to 30 minutes. Cool then cut into bars.

Estelle Dunlap

NUTTY COCONUT BARS
(A Microwave Recipe)

1 2/3 cups flour
2 Tbsp. sugar
1/2 cup margarine, softened
1/2 cup chocolate chips
3/4 cup chopped walnuts

1/2 cup white choc. chips
3/4 cup flaked coconut
1 15oz.can sweetened
   condensed skim milk

Combine flour and sugar in small bowl. Cut in margarine. Press in bottom of 11"x7" glass baking dish. Microwave on HIGH for three minutes or until set. Sprinkle both chocolate chips evenly over warm crust, then sprinkle with coconut. Pour sweetened condensed skim milk evenly over coconut and top with walnuts.

Microwave on HIGH for seven minutes. Remove and let cool several hours or overnight before cutting into bars. Makes 24 bars. 208 calories each.

Elmer Gorham

TOFFEE TOPPED BARS

2 cups brown sugar, packed
2 cups flour
1/2 cup butter or margarine
1 tsp. baking powder
1/2 tsp. salt
1 tsp. vanilla

1 cup milk
1 egg
1 cup chocolate chips
1/2 cup chopped walnuts
1/4 cup flaked coconut

In a large bowl, mix together brown sugar and flour. Cut in the butter until mixture resembles course crumbs. Remove one cup of the mixture and set aside. To the mixture in the large bowl, add baking powder and salt. Beat in vanilla, milk and egg. Continue beating until a smooth batter forms. Pour batter into a lightly greased 9"x13" pan. In a small bowl, combine chocolate chips and walnuts and fold in the coconut. Sprinkle the reserved crumb mixture over top of the batter in pan. Sprinkle with the chocolate chip mixture. Using a long, flat spatula, spread surface evenly.

Bake at 350° for 35 minutes. Transfer pan to wire rack and cool bars completely before slicing. Makes 24 bars.

Beth Few

BONBON BROWNIES

2/3 cup flour
1/4 cup cocoa
1/2 tsp. baking powder
1/2 cup shortening
1 cup sugar

2 eggs
1 tsp. vanilla
1/2 cup chopped pecans
1/4 tsp. cream of tartar
1/4 tsp. salt

(con't next page)

BONBON BROWNIES (CON'T)

Cream shortening and 3/4 cup sugar, then add one egg, one egg yolk and vanilla, beating well. Sift together flour, cocoa, baking powder and salt. Blend this mixture into the creamed mixture. Add 1/4 cup chopped pecans and mix thoroughly. Spread this mixture in a well greased 8"x8" pan. Beat one egg white with cream of tartar until foamy. Gradually add 1/4 cup sugar and beat until mixture stands in stiff peaks. Fold in 1/4 cup chopped pecans and spread this mixture over the batter.

Bake at 350° for 30 to 35 minutes until lightly browned. Cut into bars when cold.

Arvilla Hall

PEANUT BUTTER BROWNIES

1 3/4 cups flour	2 eggs
1 tsp. baking powder	1 tsp. vanilla
2/3 cup butter, softened	1/3 cup milk
3/4 cup peanut butter	2 1/2 cups chocolate
1/2 cup sugar	candy Kisses
1 cup light brown sugar, packed	1/2 tsp. shortening

In a small bowl, sift flour and baking powder and set aside. In a large bowl, cream butter and peanut butter with sugar and brown sugar until light and fluffy. Add eggs and vanilla beating well. Gradually beat in milk and flour mixture. Spread half of batter in a greased 9"x13" pan. Spread 2 cups of the kisses over the batter. Spread remaining batter over chocolate, covering completely.

Bake at 325° for 40 to 45 minutes or until toothpick comes out clean. Cool completely in pan on wire rack.

In a small microwave-safe bowl, place remaining 1/2 cup kisses and shortening (not butter, margarine or oil). Microwave on high power (100%) for 30 seconds or just until melted when stirred. Drizzle over brownies. Cut into bars.

Good Neighbor,
Dave Marmon

SAUCEPAN BROWNIES

4 sticks butter or margarine
1 cup +2 Tbsp. cocoa
3 cups sugar
6 eggs (or 1 1/2 cups egg
powder & 1 1/2 cups water
whisked together)

1 Tbsp. vanilla
2 1/4 cups flour
1 1/2 cups chocolate chips
or walnuts

In a large saucepan, melt butter or margarine. Remove immediately from heat. Stir in cocoa and sugar, mixing well. Blend in the eggs (if using dry egg mixture, be sure mixture is smooth before adding). Add vanilla. Stir in flour, a little at a time, until smooth. Add chocolate chips or walnuts. Spread into two greased 7"x11" pans or one 12"x18" pan.

Bake at 350° for 25 to 30 minutes and cool. Frost with Fudge Frosting (see below) and cut into squares. This recipe is a favorite with our friends and family who desire a moist, rich chocolate dessert. Leftovers freeze well!

Rosemary Dever

FUDGE FROSTING

1/4 cup margarine
or 1/2 cup butter, melted
1 tsp. vanilla

1/4 cup cocoa
2-3 cups confect. sugar
Hot water

In a small bowl, put the melted butter or margarine. Add cocoa and confectioners sugar. Stir in vanilla and mix with enough hot water for a desired spreading consistency. Spread on brownies.

Rosemary Dever

BROWNIES FOR A CROWD

8 1oz. squares chocolate	2 cups flour
1 1/3 cups butter or margarine	1 Tbsp. salt
4 cups sugar	1 Tbsp. vanilla
1 1/2 cups eggs (about 8)	4 cups chopped nuts

Melt chocolate and butter or margarine. Add sugar and mix. Beat in eggs. Add flour, salt, vanilla and nuts. Spread about 3/4" thick in a 10"x17" pan.

Bake at 325° for 25 to 40 minutes. Remove from oven while mixture is sticky but not doughy. Cool and cut.

Eunice Hernberger

EASY BROWNIES

Mix one box of instant chocolate pudding as directed on box plus add an extra 3 Tbsp. milk. Add one box of chocolate cake mix to pudding mixture and mix. Add 2 cups of chocolate chips and mix. Put mixture in a greased jelly roll pan.

Bake at 350° for 20 to 25 minutes. Cut when cool.

Eileen Dever

SPRINGERLE

4 eggs; 3/4 pound powdered sugar; 2 tsp. ground anise; 1/4 tsp. baking soda, dissolved in a little milk; 1 pound of flour, or enough to make the dough stiff enough to roll; use pastry flour; and butter the size of an egg.

Stir the eggs, butter and sugar 1/2 an hour, then add soda and anise and gradually the flour. Let dough rest an hour, then roll out and press into forms. Roll dough about the thickness of the little finger. Have wooden forms; after you press them on the dough, cut them out, then lay them on your board, one next to the other. Let them lay overnight in a cool place.

Bake in the morning in a moderate oven about 15 minutes.

NO BAKE CHOCOLATE CHEWS

1 cup sugar
1 cup light Karo syrup
1 cup chocolate chips

1 cup peanut butter
6 cups cereal (see below)
1 cup butterscotch chips

In a large saucepan, mix well and heat sugar and syrup. When mixture starts to bubble remove from heat immediately. Add peanut butter and stir well. Add cereal (Special K, Corn Flakes, Rice Krispies, etc.) to the mixture and mix well. Spread into a 9"x13" pan. Melt chocolate and butterscotch chips together and spread over mixture in pan. Cool completely and cut into bars. Great tasting, quick dessert for chocolate and peanut butter lovers!

Rosemary Dever

SPONGE CANDY

1 cup sugar
1 cup dark corn syrup

1 Tbsp. white vinegar
1 Tbsp. fresh baking soda

In a large saucepan, combine sugar, syrup and vinegar. Cook, stirring constantly until sugar dissolves. Then cook uncovered and without stirring until candy reaches 300° measured on a candy thermometer.
Remove pan from heat, add soda while stirring quickly and vigorously. Pour immediately into a 9x9x2 inch greased pan. Mixture will bubble and spread out and up. Cool completely on a wire rack. Break sponge into pieces.
Melt one pound Merkins chocolate and dip the sponge pieces into the melted chocolate. Put on wax paper.

Yolanda Gilchrist

CHOCOLATE MARSHMALLOW FUDGE

2 cups sugar
1 cup milk
2 squares unsweetened
  chocolate
3 Tbsp. butter

1 Tbsp. vanilla
10 marshmallows cut into
  squares or 40 miniature
  marshmallows

In saucepan, bring sugar, milk and chocolate to a soft ball stage. Remove from heat and add butter and vanilla. Fold in marshmallows and turn out into a buttered pan. Cool. Cut into squares.

Eunice Hernberger

NO BAKE CHOCOLATE OATMEAL COOKIES

2 cups sugar
1/4 lb. butter or margarine
Oats

1/2 cup milk
3/4 cup cocoa

Mix all ingredients together and boil for five minutes in a large saucepan. Add enough oats until mixture is thick. Drop on cookie sheet lined with wax paper.
Refrigerate until firm.

Maggie Lupo

PEANUT BUTTER FUDGE

2 cups sugar
2/3 cup milk
4 Tbsp. peanut butter

1 Tbsp. vanilla
Dash salt

In a saucepan, bring sugar and milk to a soft ball stage. Remove from heat and add peanut butter, vanilla and salt. Beat until creamy. Turn into a buttered pan to 3/4" deep. Cool slightly. Cut into squares with a sharp pointed knife.

Eunice Hernberger

RECIPES & NOTES

DESSERTS

&

PIES

HOME MADE
PIES
A SPECIALTY

APPLES IN THE HAY

1 1/2 cups flour	2 eggs
3 Tsp. baking soda	1 cup milk
1/2 tsp. nutmeg	1-2 tsps. cinnamon
2 to 3 cups apples, sliced	

Topping:

2 shredded wheat biscuits	1/2 cup melted butter
2 tsp. cinnamon	

Mix topping ingredients together and set aside. In a large bowl, mix flour, baking soda, nutmeg and cinnamon. Add eggs and milk mixing thoroughly. Spread mixture in a greased 10"x13" pan. Cover with apple slices and sprinkle topping over all.

Bake at 375° for 45 minutes.

Laurel Dumych

APPLE MACAROON

5 or 6 cooking apples	2 tsp. cinnamon
1/2 cup sugar	2 Tbsp. butter

Batter topping:

2 Tbsp. butter or marg.	1 egg
1/2 cup sugar	1/2 cup sifted flour

Slice apples and place in greased baking dish. Sprinkle with sugar and cinnamon and dot with butter.

Batter: Cream butter, add sugar and cream until light and fluffy. Add egg and beat. Add flour and mix well. Spoon batter over apple slices.

Bake at 350° for 45 minutes. Batter may be doubled.

Ruth Jerge

EASY BANANA TIRAMISU

1 1/2 cups milk
2 Tbsp. instant coffee grains
1 8oz.pkg. cream cheese, softened
1/4 cup sugar
1 pkg. vanilla instant pudding
2 cups thawed whipped topping

3 ripe bananas, sliced
1 6oz.pkg. ladyfingers, split and cut in half
1 1/2 oz. grated semisweet chocolate
Banana slices for garnish
Chocolate shavings for garnish

In a small bowl, stir together milk and coffee until coffee is almost dissolved. Set aside. In a large bowl, beat together cream cheese and sugar until smooth and blended. Stir in pudding mix. Gradually beat in the coffee mixture until smooth and blended. Fold in whipped topping and the three sliced bananas until just blended. Set aside.
Layer a third of the ladyfingers on bottom and sides of a three quart serving dish. Evenly spoon in a third of the cream cheese mixture and sprinkle with half of the grated chocolate. Repeat layers ending with cheese mixture. Chill at least one hour before serving. Garnish with additional banana slices and chocolate shavings.

Good Neighbor,
Dave Marmon

BREAD PUDDING

5 cups toasted stale bread crumbs
1/2 cup raisins
2 apples, sliced small
4 eggs
1/3 cup white sugar

1 tsp. cinnamon
1 tsp. vanilla
2 1/2 cups milk
1/3 cup brown sugar
Butter

(con't next page)

BREAD PUDDING (CON'T)

Mix bread crumbs, apples and raisins and place into a baking dish greased with one Tbsp. of butter. Add two Tbsp. of melted butter. Beat eggs and add white sugar, cinnamon, vanilla and milk. Pour over bread mixture. Sprinkle top with brown sugar.

Bake at 325° for about 50 to 60 minutes until custard is set. Can be served with a lemon sauce. (See next recipe)

Alma Miller

LEMON SAUCE

1/2 cup white sugar
1/2 cup brown sugar
2 Tbsp. cornstarch

1 3/4 cups water
1 Tbsp. butter
1/4 cup lemon juice

Mix all ingredients together and cook on low until sauce becomes clear and thickens. You can add slices of lemons!

Alma Miller

CHERRY COBBLER DELUXE

1 can cherry pie filling
1 8oz. can crushed pineapple,
   drained

1 box yellow or white cake
   mix
1 Tbsp. margarine

Place pie filling and pineapple in 9"x13" baking dish. Stir to mix. Sprinkle cake mix over fruit. Sprinkle 1/2 to one cup warm water over cake mix. DO NOT STIR! Dot with margarine.

Bake at 350° for 45 to 50 minutes. Serve warm with ice cream or chilled with whipped topping.

Laura Shortridge

CHOCOLATE STRAWBERRY TART

3/4 cup butter, softened
1/2 cup powdered sugar
1 1/2 cups flour
1/2 cup milk
2 egg yolks, beaten

1/4 cup sugar
1/4 tsp. salt
2 cups chocolate chips
1 pint strawberries, hulled

In a small bowl, cream butter with powdered sugar until light and fluffy. Stir in flour. Press mixture onto bottom and sides of a 9 1/2" round tart pan with removable bottom.

Bake at 350° for 20 to 25 minutes or until browned. Cool. In a microwave-safe bowl, microwave milk at high power (100%) one to two minutes until hot but not boiling. With a wire whisk, stir in egg yolks, sugar and salt. Microwave 30 seconds at a time stirring after each heating until mixture is hot, smooth and slightly thickened. Stir in chocolate chips until melted and mixture is smooth. Pour into prepared crust. Place plastic wrap directly onto surface of tart and refrigerate until firm. To serve, remove plastic wrap. Slice strawberries and arrange over top of tart. Serve chilled.

Good Neighbor,
Dave Marmon

DATE~MARSHMALLOW LOG

45 graham crackers
24 diced marshmallows or
   96 miniature marshmallows
3 cups chopped walnuts
1 1/2 cups heavy cream
1 1/2 cups chopped dates

Crush graham crackers into crumbs. Combine marshmallows, dates and nuts with 2 3/4 cups graham cracker crumbs. Add cream (not whipped). Mix thoroughly. Shape into a 3 1/2" roll. Roll in remaining crumbs. Wrap in waxed paper and chill. Cut into 3/4" slices and serve.

Eunice Hernberger

FRUIT AND RICE COMPOTE

White rice
1 can mandarin oranges
1 bag miniature marshmallows
1 can pineapple tidbits
1 jar maraschino cherries
1 cont. whipped topping

Cook rice according to how many servings you want. Drain the fruits, saving liquids. Soak marshmallows in juice until softened and drain. Combine rice and fruit. Add softened marshmallows. Stir in whipped topping (dream whip may be used). Pile into a compote and chill.
I vary the fruits with the seasons. Ex: for the 4th of July I use blueberries, strawberries and for Christmas I color the rice green, etc.

Donna May Barnes

GRAHAM CRACKER DATE ROLL

3 lbs. (6 qts.) small
   marshmallows
3 lbs. (7 1/2 cups) dates,
   cut up

3 lbs. (13 1/2 cups)
   graham cracker crumbs
3 cups chopped nuts
2 1/4 cups water

Mix and knead together all ingredients. Pack in loaf pans
or make into rolls. Refrigerate for 24 hours. Slice and
serve with whipped cream.

Eunice Hernberger

LEMON CUPS

1 cup sugar
1/4 cup flour
Dash salt
2 Tbsp. melted butter

1/3 cup lemon juice
1 1/2 cups scalded milk
3 eggs
2 tsp. grated lemon peel

Combine sugar, flour, salt and melted butter. Add lemon
peel and juice. In another bowl, slowly stir scalded milk
and three   beaten egg yolks. Add to first mixture. Fold in
three stiff-beaten egg whites. Pour 2/3 full into custard
cups or casserole dish. Set dish or cups into pan filled with
one inch of hot water.

Bake at 325° for 45 minutes or until sponge cake on top is
done. Serve warm or chilled. Note: The mixture forms a
sponge cake topping and sauce bottom while baking.

Eunice Hernberger

LEBKUCHEN

*1 pint of syrup or honey; 1/4 pound sugar; 1 tsp.
cinnamon; 1/2 tsp. ginger; 1 tsp. ground anise;
1/4 pound almonds, chopped fine; 1 liquor glass
of brandy; 1 1/4 pound of flour or enough to
make the dough stiff enough; butter about the size
of an egg; a good pinch of nutmeg; 1/4 pound of
citron. Boil the syrup or honey, then add the
sugar and all the rest, flour last. Roll dough out
and cut in squares or any plain form of cutter, and
bake slowly!*

POTS DE CREME

6 oz.(1c.) semi-sweet chocolate
  chips
2 Tbsp. sugar
1 cup heavy cream

3 egg yolks
1 pkg. dessert pastry
  shells

Melt chocolate chips slowly in top of double boiler. Stir in sugar and 1/2 cup heavy cream and cook, stirring constantly until very smooth. Beat egg yolks. Slowly add chocolate mixture, a little at a time so as not to curdle the yolks, and continue beating the mixture until eggs and chocolate are combined. Set aside and let cool to room temperature. Whip 1/2 cup heavy cream, and when the chocolate mixture has cooled, fold in the whipped cream. Pour mixture into dessert pastry shells and refrigerate until serving. (To be sure that pastry shells do not become soggy, do not fill them too far in advance of serving.) Serves 6.

Mary Lou Hallatt

PUMPKIN SQUARES

Crust:
1 3/4 cups graham cracker
  crumbs
1/3 cup sugar
1/2 cup melted butter

2 eggs
3/4 cup sugar
1 8oz. pkg. cream cheese

Topping:
1 (16oz.) can pumpkin
3 egg yolks (save whites)
1/2 cup sugar
1/2 tsp. salt
1/2 cup milk

2 tsp. cinnamon
1 env. unflavored gelatin
1/4 cup cold water
1/4 cup sugar

(con't next page)

PUMPKIN SQUARES (CON'T)

Crust:
Mix cracker crumbs and 1/3 cup sugar. Stir in melted butter. Pat into a 9"x13" pan. Beat 2 eggs, 3/4 cup sugar and cream cheese until light and fluffy. Pour over cracker mixture.
Bake at 350° for 20 minutes.
Topping:
Beat pumpkin, egg yolks, 1/2 cup sugar, milk, salt and cinnamon in the top of a double boiler. Cook, stirring frequently until thick (about five minutes). In saucepan with 1/4 cup cold water, sprinkle unflavored gelatin and stir until dissolved. Beat egg whites until foamy, gradually beating in 1/4 cup sugar and continue beating until stiff. Fold in pumpkin mixture. Pour over crust. Refrigerate. Garnish with whipped cream when serving.

Beth Strablow

SPICED PEACHES

1 14oz. can peach halves   1/4 tsp. nutmeg
3 cloves   1/4 tsp. cinnamon

Pour canned peaches into a shallow dish. Add cloves, cinnamon and nutmeg. Microwave on high until heated or heat carefully in a saucepan. May be served warm or chilled.
These taste almost like the canned spiced peaches I used to can when younger and more energetic!

Donna May Barnes

APPLE PIE SQUARES

3 3/4 cups flour
1 1/2 tsp. salt
3/4 cup shortening
3 eggs, beaten
1/3 cup milk
8 cups sliced apples

1 1/2 cups sugar
1 tsp. cinnamon
1/2 tsp. nutmeg
1 cup cornflakes
1 egg white, beaten

Combine flour and salt. Cut in shortening until mixture resembles course crumbs. Add eggs and milk and mix to form dough. Chill for 20 minutes. Divide dough in half. Roll one half to fit bottom and sides of greased 10"x15" pan. Arrange apples over crust. Combine sugar, cinnamon and nutmeg and cornflakes. Sprinkle this mixture over the apples. Roll remaining dough to fit top of pan and place over the apples. Seal edges. Cut slits in top. Brush with egg white.

Bake at 400° for 15 minutes. Reduce heat to 350° and bake for 25 to 30 minutes more. Cool and slice.

Good as is or frost with a thin butter cream frosting. Serves 20.

Patricia O. Few

CRAZY CRUST APPLE PIE

1 cup flour
2 Tbsp. sugar
1 tsp. baking powder
Filling:
1 can apple pie filling (or cherry)
1 Tbsp. lemon juice
1/2 tsp. cinnamon or apple pie spice

3/4 cup water
2/3 cup shortening
1 egg
1/2 tsp. salt

Combine above ingredients. Blend well and then beat for two to three minutes. Spread batter in 9" or 10" pie plate. Mix filling ingredients and carefully spoon into center of batter. Do Not Stir!

Bake at 425° for 40 minutes until crust is golden brown.

Ann Dumych

AMARETTO CHOCOLATE PIE

1 3.4 oz.pkg. cook & serve
   chocolate pudding
1 2/3 cup milk
1/3 cup amaretto

1 graham cracker pie crust
1 pkg.dream whip topping
1 tsp. amaretto

Cook pudding and pie filling mix with milk until thick. Add 1/3 cup amaretto and stir well. Pour into pie shell and cover with plastic wrap. Refrigerate until cold. Remove wrap. Whip dream whip as per directions and stir in 1 tsp. amaretto. Spread this mixture on top of pie. May be garnished with sliced almonds.

Jan Robarr

CHOCOLATE PEANUT PIE

Crust:
1 cup crushed vanilla wafers
1/4 cup melted butter
Layer #1:
4 oz. cream cheese, softened
3 Tbsp. peanut butter
1/2 cup sifted powdered sugar
Layer #2:
1 pkg. instant choc. pudding
Topping:
1 cup whipped topping
Grated chocolate

1/3 cup chopped peanuts

1 cup whipped topping
1 banana, thinly sliced

1 1/2 cups milk

3-4 Tbsp. chopped peanuts

Combine crust ingredients and press into a sprayed or buttered 9" pie plate. Bake at 375° for 10 minutes. Mix layer #1 ingredients, except banana and pour into crust. Arrange banana slices on top. Layer #2: Prepare pudding mix with the milk and beat two minutes. Spread evenly over pie.
Topping: Spread on whipped topping and sprinkle with peanuts and chocolate.

Ruth Jerge

LEMON MERINGUE PIE

10" baked pie shell
1/4 cup cornstarch
3 Tbsp. flour
1 3/4 cup sugar
1 3/4 cup hot water
1/4 tsp. salt
1 tsp. vanilla

1/2 cup lemon juice
1 Tbsp. grated lemon rind
1 Tbsp. butter
4 eggs
1/4 tsp. cream of tartar
1/2 cup sugar

Combine cornstarch, 1 3/4 cup sugar, flour and salt. Gradually add water, stirring until smooth. Bring to a boil and boil one minute. Stir some of hot mixture into four slightly beaten egg yolks. Return to hot mixture and cook over low heat for five minutes. Remove from heat and stir in juice, lemon rind and butter. Pour into cooled pie shell.
Beat four egg whites with cream of tartar until frothy. Gradually beat in 1/2 cup sugar, a little at a time. Beat at high speed until stiff. Add vanilla before beating is finished. Put on top of filling.
Bake in a pre-heated 400° oven until nicely browned. Watch carefully so that peaks do not burn!

Ruth Jerge

FRESH PEACH PARFAIT PIE

1 3oz.pkg. peach gelatin
1/2 cup boiling water
2 cups finely chopped peaches
1 cup sliced peaches

1/4 cup sugar
1/2 tsp. almond extract
4 oz. whipped topping
1 baked pie crust

Mix gelatin with boiling water. In a one quart measuring cup, chop fresh peaches finely until you have two cups. Add one cup of sliced peaches, sugar and almond flavoring. Mix with gelatin. When it becomes quite thick, add whipped topping, thawed. Turn into crust. Refrigerate overnight.

Anna B. Wallace

PECAN PIE

3 eggs
1/2 cup sugar
1 cup light Karo syrup

1 Tbsp. vanilla
1 heaping cup pecan
  halves

Mix all ingredients well and pour into an unbaked pastry shell.
Bake at 325° for 50 minutes.
This is an old family favorite!

Joan Pearson

AUNT VIOLET'S PECAN TARTS

1 stick margarine
3 oz. cream cheese
1 cup flour
1 tsp. vanilla

1 Tbsp. margarine
3/4 cup dark brown sugar
1 egg
2/3 cup crushed pecans

Mix together stick of margarine, cream cheese and flour. Refrigerate overnight. Divide into 24 balls. Shape into miniature muffin pans. Mix together pecans, one Tbsp. margarine, brown sugar, egg and vanilla. Fill tart shells.
Bake at 350° for 25 minutes. Remove from tins immediately. These freeze well!

Christa Caldwell

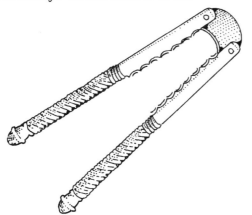

PUMPKIN PIE
(FARM RICH-NO CHOLESTEROL)

1 16oz.can pumpkin
3/4 cup Farm Rich (reg.or light)
3/4 cup brown sugar
1/2 cup egg substitute

2 tsp. pumpkin pie spice
1/2 tsp. salt
1 9" deep dish pie shell,
  unbaked

Pour pumpkin, farm rich, brown sugar, egg substitute, and spices into a blender and process at medium speed for 2 minutes. Pour into pie shell.

Bake in preheated oven at 425° for 15 minutes. Reduce heat to 350 and continue to bake for 30 to 40 minutes more or until a knife inserted near center comes out clean.

Virginia Strablow

SHOWY STRAWBERRY PIE

1 cup sugar
2 Tbsp. cornstarch
Dash Salt
1 qt. strawberries

1 cup water
4 Tbsp. strawberry jello
  powder
1 pie shell, baked

Combine sugar, cornstarch and salt. Add water and cook until clear. Add jello and stir until dissolved. Cool. Cut berries. Add berries and pour into baked shell. Top with whipped cream if desired.

Arvilla Hall

BREAD PIE
Soak 1 slice of very light bread in a pint of rich milk. When it is quite soft, beat it smooth. Add one egg, well beaten and 4 Tbsp. sugar. Flavor with nutmeg.
Pour into a rich crust and bake.

RECIPES & NOTES

RECIPES & NOTES

MAIN DISHES

BEAN & FRANK SANDWICHES

6 hotdog buns
1 can bean & bacon condensed
  soup
2 Tbsp. sweet pickle relish

6 hotdogs
1/3 cup water
1/4 cup catsup

Toast hotdog buns and place on cookie sheet. Split hotdogs lengthwise and place on buns. Combine soup, water, catsup and relish. Spoon this mixture evenly over hotdogs.
Bake at 350° until hot and bubbly. Kids favorite!

Donna May Barnes

MAKE AHEAD BREAKFAST CASSEROLE

4 cups plain croutons
8 oz. shredded cheddar cheese
8 eggs (or eggbeaters)
4 cups milk

1 tsp. prepared mustard
1/4 tsp. onion powder
Pepper to taste

Mix croutons and cheese together in bottom of greased 9"x13" pan. Combine the rest of the ingredients and pour over crouton mixture.
Bake at 350°until set, 55 to 60 minutes. This can be made ahead and frozen. To bake, thaw, cover and reheat.

Christa Caldwell

BREAKFAST CASSEROLE

12 slices white bread, cubed   1 lb. bacon
2 cups grated sharp cheese   8 large eggs
1 lb. bulk sausage   4 cups milk

Fry sausage, drain and crumble. Fry bacon until crisp and crumble. Butter an 11"x14" pan. Put half of the bread cubes on the bottom. Add half of the cheese, then the sausage and bacon. Add remaining bread and cheese. Beat eggs with the milk and pour over all. Refrigerate for 24 hours.
Bake at 325° for 45 minutes. Bread is easier to cube if frozen. This recipe can be prepared, then frozen.

Maggie Lupo

JACK'S BREAKFAST OATMEAL

Plain oatmeal can be referred to as "cruel gruel"! The following works well in a microwave, but can be done stove-top if you prefer:

In a microwave container, add:
1/2 cup oatmeal   1/4 tsp. cinnamon
One shake of salt   1 cup water
1 Tbsp. brown sugar

Stir ingredients and start cooking. On high, cook for two minutes and 15 seconds. Stir and restart for another minute and a half. Let sit for a couple of minutes. Add milk, and if your doctor allows it, add a bit of cream or a palatable substitute.
To enhance the enjoyment, add a couple of slices of buttered toast (jam optional).

Jack Dickenson

TOAD IN THE HOLE CASSEROLE

5 eggs
1 1/2 cups flour
1 tsp. baking soda

3 Tbsp. melted butter
Milk
1 pkg. frozen sausage links

Beat well, eggs, flour, baking soda and butter. Spread frozen sausage (or you may brown fresh sausage) in the bottom of an oiled 10"x13" glass pan. Pour batter over top. Bake at 425° for 25 to 30 minutes or until it is fluffy and golden brown. Serve immediately. Good with butter!

Laurel Dumych

CALICO CASSEROLE

1 pkg. frozen mixed vegetables
 (canned may be used)
1 Tbsp. butter
1 slice bread, cubed (3/4 cup)
1/4 cup flour
Dash pepper
1/4 tsp. salt
1/2 tsp. dry mustard

1/2 tsp. Worcestershire
 sauce
1 1/2 cups milk
3 Tbsp. butter
1 Tbsp. minced onion
1 cup grated ched. cheese
1/2 lb. cooked ham, cut in
 strips 1 1/2" x 1/4"

Cook vegetables as directed. Melt 1 Tbsp. butter and toss with bread cubes. Set aside. In same saucepan, melt 3 Tbsp. butter and stir in flour, salt, pepper, mustard and Worcestershire sauce. Add milk. Cook over low heat until smooth and thickened, stirring often. Add onion and cheese. Cook, stirring often until cheese is melted. Add drained vegetables and ham. Pour into 9"x5"x2"baking dish. Sprinkle with bread cubes.
Bake at 350° for 30 minutes or until heated through.

Inez Metz

(97)

FAMILY FAVORITE CASSEROLE

1/4 lb. sliced fresh mushrooms
   or 1 6oz. can, drained
1 cup chopped onion
1/4 cup chopped green pepper
1/3 cup margarine
1/4 cup flour
1/8 tsp. salt
2 cups canned tomatoes
1/4 cup shredded parmesan
   cheese

1 clove garlic, crushed
1 cup milk
1 8oz.pkg. elbow macaroni
1/2 lb. processed sharp
   cheddar cheese such as
   Old English
1 9 1/4 oz. can white tuna
   packed in water
1/4 cup buttered bread
   crumbs

Cook, rinse and drain macaroni and set aside. Sauté onions and green pepper in margarine until tender. Add mushrooms and sauté one to two minutes longer. Blend in flour with some of the liquid from the canned tomatoes and cook, stirring until mixture thickens. Add tomatoes with liquid and milk gradually, stirring constantly until mixture thickens. Add salt, macaroni. Cube the cheese and add, drain the tuna, flake it and add. Stir to mix. Pour into a 2 1/2 quart greased baking dish. Mix parmesan cheese and buttered bread crumbs and sprinkle over the top of the casserole.

Bake at 350° until hot and bubbly, 25 to 30 minutes.
Makes eight generous servings. Good served with gelatin or chef salad and garlic bread.

Joan Pearson

CHILI CON CARNE

1 lb. ground beef
1 medium onion, chopped
1 can kidney beans
1 can tomato soup

Salt, pepper, chili powder
   to taste
1/4green pepper, chopped
1 clove garlic

Brown onion, pepper, garlic and beef. Add kidney beans and soup. Add seasonings to taste. Simmer about 30 minutes. Very easy and good too!

Inez Metz

EGGS A LA KING

2 Tbsp. salad oil
1/4 cup chopped green pepper
1/4 cup chopped onion
1 cup chopped celery
1 can condensed cream of
  celery soup

1/2 cup milk
1 cup processed American
  cheese, diced
4 hard cooked eggs,
  chopped
6 green olives, sliced

Heat the oil in a large frying pan, then sauté the green pepper, onion and celery until nearly tender. Add the soup, milk and cheese. Heat, stirring until cheese melts. Stir in chopped eggs and olives and heat thoroughly. Serve over hot, buttered toast.

Virginia Strablow

ZUCCHINI LASAGNA

1 lb. mild Italian sausage
1/2 cup chopped onion
1 15oz.can tomato sauce
1/2 cup water
1/4 tsp. salt
1/4 tsp. oregano
12 oz. mozzarella cheese, sliced

7 lasagna noodles, cooked
  & drained
3/4 cup grated parmesan
  cheese
2 Tbsp. flour
4 cups zucchini slices

Brown sausage with onion and drain. Stir in tomato sauce, water and seasonings. Simmer 30 minutes. Stir occasionally. Combine parmesan cheese and flour. Layer half the noodles on bottom of buttered 8 3/4"x13 1/2" baking dish. Top with half the zucchini, half the parmesan cheese mixture, half the meat sauce and half of the mozzarella cheese. Repeat layers except the mozz. cheese.
Bake at 375° for 20 to 25 minutes until zucchini is tender. Add remaining mozzarella cheese and return to oven and bake until cheese begins to melt. Let stand 10 minutes before serving.
Serves 6.

Virginia Strablow

MACARONI & CHEESE

3 1/2 cups cooked elbow
  macaroni
1/4 cup chopped pimento
3/4 cup milk
3 Tbsp. chopped onion
1/4 tsp. pepper

1 tsp. Worcestershire
  sauce
1 1/4 cups American
cheese (cubed Velveeta
  works best)
2 tsp. dry mustard

Put cooked macaroni in a 1 1/2 qt. casserole dish. Put the rest of the ingredients in a saucepan and cook over low heat until cheese is melted. Pour over the macaroni and top with four slices of cheese. This will form a bubbly crust.
Bake at 350° for 25 minutes.

Donna May Barnes

MAKE AHEAD MIRACLE MEAT ROLLS

1 1/2 lbs. ground round
1 egg
1/4 cup dry bread crumbs
1 tsp. salt
2 cups mashed potatoes

1/3 cup salad dressing
1/3 cup parmesan cheese
1/4 cup chopped celery
2 Tbsp. chopped onion
2 chopped hardboiled eggs

Combine ground round, egg, bread crumbs and salt. Pat the mixture into a 8"x14" rectangle on wax paper. Combine the rest of the ingredients and spread mixture over meat. Roll up as for a jelly roll. Chill overnight. Slice and place on broiler rack.
Bake 350° for 25-30 minutes.

Donna May Barnes

GREEK PASTA WITH TOMATOES & BEANS

2 14oz. cans diced tomatoes
  with basil, garlic & oregano
1 19oz. can cannellini beans,
  rinsed & drained
1 10oz.bag fresh spinach, chopped

4 cups hot, cooked penne
  pasta
1/2 cup crumbled feta
  cheese

Combine tomatoes and beans in a large nonstick skillet and simmer for 10 minutes. Add spinach and cook two minutes or until spinach wilts, stirring occasionally. Place one cup pasta on each of four plates. Top each serving with 1 1/4 cups of the sauce and two Tbsp. cheese. You can also add grated Romano or parmesan at the table. Low cal and very good!

Patricia O. Few

BURRITO PIE

4 tortilla shells
1/2 lb. ground beef
1 medium onion, diced
8 oz. refried beans
1/3 cup taco sauce

1/2 cup chopped peppers
Garlic powder
Chili powder
2 cups shredded jack
  cheese

Fry tortilla shells in hot oil for 30 seconds on each side until blistered. Place on paper towel. Cook beef, onion and peppers. Season with spices to taste. Add beans and taco sauce and remove from heat. Place one tortilla in a pie pan. Top with 1/4 of the meat mixture and 1/2 cup Monterey Jack cheese, then another tortilla and another 1/4 cup of meat and 1/2 cup of cheese until it is all layered.

Sherry Bauer

PASTA PRIMAVERA

4 cloves garlic, minced
6 Tbsp. extra virgin olive oil
1 medium onion, diced
1 cup chopped broccoli
1/2 cup green & red pepper, diced
1 cup diced tomatoes
1 cup sliced mushrooms
Salt to taste
Fresh ground pepper
Basil to taste
1/4 cup white balsamic vinegar
1 lb. cooked pasta, al dente
Fresh grated Romano or parmesan cheese
Crushed red pepper

In a large frying pan, sauté garlic in olive oil until cooked through. Add onion and sauté until clear. Add all vegetables, salt, pepper and basil and sauté on medium heat until vegetables are barely tender. Add vinegar to mixture and sauté one to two minutes more. Pour vegetable mixture over hot pasta. Season to taste with cheese and crushed red pepper.
Bon Appetite!! Serves 4.

Dr. August J. Domenico,
Dr. David J. Lewis of
Lockport Chiropractic

HERB CRUST PIZZA

4 cups warm water
4 pkg. dry yeast
1/4 cup sugar
Olive oil
Mozzarella cheese
1 Tbsp. salt
2 Tbsp. Italian seasoning
8 cups flour
Pepperoni

Mix dough and let rest for 15 minutes. Grease pizza pan. Spread dough with the back of a spoon. Add your favorite pizza sauce. Sprinkle with oregano and add a few sprinkles of olive oil. Add meat and cheese and anything else desired. Bake at 425° for 15 to 20 minutes.

Patricia O. Few

GREEK FRESH TOMATO PIZZA

2 medium tomatoes
3 6" pita pockets
1 egg white
1 tsp. water
1 Tbsp. salad oil
1 cup shredded mozzarella
  cheese

1 cup thinly sliced green
  peppers
1/2 cup crumbled feta
  cheese
1/3 cup ripe olives, halved
1/2 tsp. oregano

Core tomatoes, slice in 1/4" slices and set aside. Split each pita to form two circles each and set aside. In a small bowl, lightly beat the egg white and water. On a 12" pizza pan arrange pita circles overlapping slightly to form a crust. Lightly brush egg white mixture under overlapped sections and press down.

Bake at 400° three to four minutes and remove from oven. Using a metal spatula press down warm pitas so they will hold together and return them to the oven. Bake until crisp, three to four more minutes longer. Lightly brush crust with oil and sprinkle with the mozzarella cheese. Arrange green pepper and tomato slices over cheese, overlapping slightly. Sprinkle with the feta cheese, olives and oregano. Bake until tomatoes are softened and cheese is melted.

Elmer Gorham

ROLL~UPS

1 pkg. flour tortillas
Tomato salsa
Black Olives

Cream cheese
Scallions
Shredded cheese

Spread tortillas with cream cheese first, then salsa. Sprinkle with chopped olives and scallions and shredded cheese. Roll up tight in wax paper and let set overnight in refrigerator. Cut in any size and serve.
Note: Either flour or corn tortillas may be used.

Florence Smith

MEXICAN QUESADILLAS

Flour tortillas
Chopped fresh tomatoes
Chopped red & green pepper
Chopped sweet onions
Mexican salsa

Sliced mushrooms
Cheddar or Mozzarella
  cheese
2 tsp. margarine
Spices as desired

Melt margarine in hot skillet. Put tortilla on top of it. Add vegetables as desired and top with cheese. Place another tortilla on top and cook until brown on the bottom. Flip tortilla and brown on the other side. Remove and cut with a pizza cutter into eight wedges. Dip in salsa. Use as an appetizer or entree.

Elmer Gorham

QUICHE

1 1/2 cups grated Swiss
  cheese
8 slices cooked bacon,
  crumbled
9" pastry shell, chilled
3 eggs, slightly beaten

1/2 tsp. dry mustard
1 cup heavy cream
1/2 cup milk
1/2 tsp. salt
1/4 tsp. pepper

Sprinkle cheese and bacon in pastry shell. Blend remaining ingredients and pour over cheese mixture.

Bake at 375° for 45 minutes or until knife inserted in center comes out clean. Cut in wedges and serve hot.

NOTE: Using a very good quality cheese will insure the success of this dish. Wonderful supper with a fresh, green salad!

Unknown

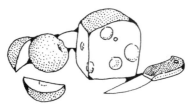

RECIPES & NOTES

RECIPES & NOTES

MEAT, POULTRY

&

SEAFOOD

BAKED ROUNDSTEAK WITH MUSHROOMS

1 1/2 - 2 lbs. boneless
  round steak
1 Tbsp. soft margarine

1 pkg. onion soup mix
1 4.5oz. jar sliced
  mushrooms, drained

Preheat oven to 350°. Place 2 long strips of foil on large cookie sheet or roasting pan. Overlap sides of foil. Place round steak on foil in center of pan. Smear margarine on steak and sprinkle with dry soup mix. Top with drained mushrooms. Fold foil loosely over steak forming a "tent". Bake for one hour to an hour and a half depending on size of the steak. Serves six to eight.

Laura Shortridge

ROAST BEEF
The sirloin is the nicest piece for roasting. Baste it frequently and bake slowly at first. Then move it nearer the fire and brown it a little at the last. In helping, see that every person has a piece of the tender-loin. The gravy should not be thick or greasy and is improved by adding a little ketchup.

BARBECUE CHUCK ROAST

3-4 lb. chuck roast
1 green pepper, chopped
1 Tbsp. salt
1 Tbsp. prepared mustard

1 onion, chopped
Large jar chili sauce
2 Tbsp. vinegar
2 Tbsp. pickling spice in
  bag

Cook the roast for approximately four hours until very tender. Saving the juice, shred the meat and set aside.
In a sauce pan put all ingredients including meat juices except the meat. Stir until smooth. Add shredded meat and spice bag. Heat through. Remove bag just before serving. Serve on rolls.

Florence Smith

CAMPFIRE STEAK

2 lbs. steak (lean chuck,
  round, etc.)
2 stalks celery, julienned
2 Tbsp. margarine

1 pkg. onion soup mix
3 carrots, quartered
3 medium potatoes, halved
1/2 tsp. salt

Place steak on large sheet of foil. Sprinkle with onion soup mix. Top with carrot, celery and potatoes. Dot with margarine and sprinkle with salt. Wrap well in foil (use several layers and wrap separately). Cook buried in hot coals for one to one and a half hours. This may be cooked on a grill or in the oven at 450°.

CROCKPOT PEPPER STEAK

2 lbs. lean round steak
2 Tbsp. flour
1/2 cup soy sauce
2 stalks celery, chopped
2 large green peppers, diced

Oil for sautéing
1 cup beef stock/bouillon
2 large onions, cut up
2 tomatoes, cut up
Cooked rice or noodles

Cut steak into thin strips and sauté in oil until browned. Stir in flour and mix well to coat the meat. Add beef stock and soy sauce. Put this in crock pot and add the rest of the ingredients. Cover and cook low for four to six hours or high for two to three hours. Serve over rice or noodles. This may be cooked on stove if carefully watched.

both recipes by Donna May Barnes

SWISS STEAK SUPREME

ANY AMOUNTS: Cut up round steak and place in a 9x12inch baking dish. Cover with a pkg. of onion soup mix, green pepper cut into strips and mushrooms. Pour on one can tomatoes, adding one Tbsp. cornstarch to the juice. Sprinkle on A1 Sauce and cover with a tinfoil tent.
Bake at 350° two to three hours.

Florence Smith

STIR-FRY STEAK

1 lb. lean top round steak
1 green pepper, chopped
1 Tbsp. cornstarch

1 onion, chopped
1 Tbsp. cooking sherry
1 Tbsp. soy sauce

Thinly slice round steak (will slice easier if partly frozen). Combine sherry, cornstarch and soy sauce and toss with meat. marinade 15 to 20 minutes. Stir fry with vegetables. I always make extra as my husband likes it for sandwiches the next day.

Donna May Barnes

CHINESE BEEF AND RICE

1 1/3 cups uncooked rice
3 cups boiling water
1 Tbsp. soy sauce
4 stalks celery, chopped
3 cups diced, cooked beef

1/4 cup oil
2 beef bouillon cubes
2 onions, diced
2 green peppers, diced

Brown rice in oil. Add water, bouillon cubes and soy sauce and simmer for 20 minutes. Add rest of ingredients and cook for 10 minutes.

Sherry Bauer

ONE DISH BEEF DINNER

IN A DUTCH OVEN: Brown individual pieces of beef (stew meat, etc.) Sprinkle with flour and top with sliced onions. Salt and pepper to taste and add 1/2 cup water.
Cook in the oven at 325° until tender. Add carrots, potatoes and water to cover. Cook until done or you are ready to eat. You may need to thicken juices for gravy.

Mary Newhard

CHUCKWAGON STEW

2 lbs. lean stew beef in small
   cubes
2 Tbsp. vegetable oil
1 tsp. sugar
2 tsp. flour
2 tsp. seasoned salt
1/4 tsp. pepper
1 tsp. chili powder
6 carrots, sliced
1 cup fresh peas

1/4 tsp. whole thyme
1 bay leaf
1 can stewed tomatoes
1 green pepper, diced
1 onion, diced
1 can beef bouillon or
   consommé
6 potatoes, large cubes
3 or 4 stalks celery, sliced

Brown meat slowly in oil in Dutch oven. Put in onion and green pepper. Add sugar and continue browning until meat is well seared. Dust lightly with flour and brown carefully. Add seasonings, bay leaf, tomatoes and bouillon. Cover and simmer over low heat until meat is almost tender, about two hours. Add the vegetables (if using frozen peas add later). Cook stew about 30 to 45 minutes or until vegetables are tender. Makes 6 servings. May be doubled!
Submitted by Melissa Dunlap in memory of her mom Elaine Koral. This was one of her most requested dinners!

Elaine Koral
Melissa Dunlap

POT ROAST

1/4 cup flour
1 tsp. dried thyme
1/2 tsp. salt
1/4 tsp. pepper
3-4 lbs. beef eye round roast
1 Tbsp. Canola oil
1 reg. size oven roasting bag

1 1/2 cups carrots, cut up
2 onions, quartered
2 ribs celery, cut into 1/2"
   pieces
1 cup red wine
1 cup beef broth
1 env. onion soup mix

(con't next page)

POT ROAST (CON'T)

In a large plastic bag, combine flour, thyme, salt and pepper. Then add the roast. Toss until completely coated. Remove the roast and set aside. Heat oil in a large pot. Add roast, cook two to three minutes per side. Combine carrots, onions and celery with the reserved flour mix in the plastic bag. Place this mixture and the roast in the oven roasting bag. Combine wine, broth and soup mix and add to the bag. Seal bag and place in a large roasting pan. Make several slits in the bag.

Bake at 350° for three hours. Allow the meat to stand 10 minutes before slicing.

Yolanda Gilchrist

SAVORY ITALIAN POT ROAST
(Pressure Cooker)

3 1/2 to 4 lbs. chuck pot roast
2 Tbsp. cooking oil
1 cup water
1 8 oz. can tomato sauce
1/2 cup dry red wine
1 carrot, finely chopped
1 3 oz. can mushrooms,
   chopped
1 Tbsp. minced onion
1 tsp. salt
1 tsp. beef bouillon powder
1 bay leaf
1/4 cup cornstarch
1/2 cup cold water
Parsley

Brown roast in hot oil. Combine 1 cup water, tomato sauce, wine, carrot, undrained mushrooms, onion, salt, bouillon and bay leaf. Pour over meat. Close cover and place over heat. Bring pressure to 15#. Cook 30 minutes. Remove from heat and bring pressure down quickly by running cold water down the outside of the cooker. Remove meat after pressure is down. Keep warm. Skim off any excess fat. Blend cornstarch and cold water and stir into pan juices. Cook until bubbly.

Ruth Jerge

BAKED PORK CHOPS

4 thick pork chops
2 Tbsp. brown sugar
1/2 tsp. pepper
Juice of 1/2 lemon
1/2 cup water
1/3 cup diced celery
1/2 tsp. salt
1/2 tsp. mustard
2 cans tomato sauce

Brown chops in fat. Place in shallow, greased baking dish. Add the rest of the ingredients and cover.
Bake at 350° for 1 1/4 hours or until chops are tender.

Ruth Jerge

OVEN BARBECUE

3 lbs. pork spareribs (I use country style-more meat)
1 lb. Italian sausage (part hot and part mild)
1 chicken fryer or parts of your choice
3 medium onions, sliced

SAUCE:
3/4 cup ketchup or chili sauce
3/4 cup water
1 Tbsp. salt
Garlic powder or minced garlic
1 Tbsp. brown sugar
2 Tbsp. white vinegar
2 Tbsp. Worcestershire sauce
2 Tbsp. lemon juice
1 tsp. chili powder
1 tsp. paprika
1/2 tsp. hot pepper sauce
1/2 tsp. pepper
Pinch oregano
Pinch sweet basil

Cut ribs into 2-rib portions (country style already small). Put in Dutch oven and cover with water. Add Italian sausage and simmer for 15 minutes. Discard water. Place chicken pieces in a roaster. Add the ribs and sausage. Spread onions over top. Combine sauce ingredients and pour over. Cover.
Bake at 325° to 350° for 1 1/2 to 2 hours or more or until done.

Ruth Jerge

(110)

PORK CHOP EXTRAVAGANZA

12 pork chops
14 potatoes
2 bunches of carrots
1 soup can of milk

1 pkg. onion soup mix
2 cans cream soup (celery,
  mushroom or chicken)

Spread browned chops on bottom of pan. Mix soups and milk in a bowl. Spread some on the meat. Cut potatoes (peeled) into wedges and layer them in pan. Spread on some soup mixture. Peel carrots, cut them in half and layer them on top of the potatoes. Spread the rest of the soup mixture. Cover pan tightly with foil.

Bake at 350° for 2 to 3 hours if chops are thick or 1 1/2 hours for thin chops.

Kathy L. Beder

BEEF BALLS

Mince very fine a piece of tender beef, fat and lean. Mince an onion with some boiled parsley. Add grated bread crumbs and season with pepper, salt and grated nutmeg and lemon peel. Mix altogether and moisten with a well-beaten egg. Roll each ball into flour and fry. Serve with a brown gravy.

PORK SHOULDER CHOPS

4 1/2" pork loin blade chops
2 Tbsp. butter or margarine
1 tsp. salt
4 small tomatoes, cut in wedges

1 medium zucchini, sliced
2 medium onions
2 to 3 tsp. sugar
1/2 tsp. leaf tarragon *

Melt butter in large skillet. Brown chops on both sides. Season with salt and top with tomatoes and zucchini. Slice onions 1/4" thick and separate into rings. Place these on top of zucchini. Sprinkle seasonings over all. Cover and cook over low heat approximately 40 minutes. Makes 4 servings.

*1/2 tsp. basil could be substituted.

Virginia Strablow

STIR~FRIED PORK

3/4 lb. boneless pork
3 Tbsp. cornstarch
4 Tbsp. soy sauce
1/2 tsp. garlic powder
1/4 tsp. ginger
1 tsp. sugar

1 cup water
2 tsp. oil
2 medium onions
2 stalks celery, sliced
1 green pepper
3 small tomatoes

Cut pork into thin strips. Combine 1 Tbsp. each cornstarch and soy sauce with spice and sugar. Add pork and let stand 15 minutes. Combine water with 2 Tbsp. cornstarch and 3 Tbsp. soy sauce and set aside. Heat 1 tsp. oil in fry pan. Add pork and stir-fry until golden. Remove. Cut onions, green pepper and tomatoes into 1" squares. Heat remaining oil in pan and add vegetables except tomatoes. Stir-fry until tender crisp. Stir in pork mix and tomatoes and cook until heated through. Before serving, add the soy sauce cornstarch mixture and heat until slightly thickened. Serve over rice.

Sherry Bauer

BAKED CHICKEN BREASTS

4 large chicken breasts, boned
and cut in half
3 Tbsp. butter or margarine
2 cans cream of chicken soup
or mushroom or one of each
1 cup dry white wine

3 Tbsp. grated parm. cheese
1 cup grated Swiss cheese
1 cup Pepperidge Farm
stuffing
3 Tbsp. chopped parsley
1 cup sour cream

Combine soup, wine, sour cream and heat almost to boiling. Remove from heat and stir in parmesan cheese. Melt butter and brown chicken breasts and place in a baking dish. Pour sauce over chicken.

Bake at 350° until chicken is tender. Cover with Swiss cheese and stuffing and sprinkle with parsley. Bake 10 to 15 minutes more until cheese is melted and crumbs brown.

Ruth Jerge

CHICKEN A LA KING

1/3 cup margarine	Dash cayenne pepper
1/2 lb. sliced mushrooms	1 1/2 cups chicken stock*
1/4 cup cornstarch	1 cup light cream
1 tsp. salt	2 cups cooked chicken,
1/4 tsp. white pepper	diced
1/4 tsp. dry mustard	1/2 cup chopped pimento

In pan, melt margarine and add mushrooms. Cook until tender, about 5 minutes. Blend in cornstarch, salt, pepper, mustard and cayenne. Remove from heat and gradually add chicken stock and light cream, stirring until smooth. Cook over medium heat until mixture thickens and comes to a boil. Boil 1 minute. Add chicken, pimento. Worcestershire sauce and 2 Tbsp. sherry may be added if desired.
*2 chicken bouillon cubes dissolved in 1 1/2 cups boiling water may be used instead.

Ruth Jerge

CHICKEN PIE

CRUST:

1/2 stick very cold butter	3 Tbsp. ice water
1 1/2 cups flour	Pinch Salt

FILLING:

1 cup mushrooms	1 each chopped red and
1 small onion, chopped	green pepper
4 Tbsp. butter	1/2 tsp. curry powder
3 Tbsp. flour	1 cup chicken stock
3/4 cup heavy cream	Salt & pepper to taste
2 to 3 cups cooked chicken, cubed	

In a food processor make crust as follows: Process cold butter, flour and salt a few turns until like pie crust. Add ice water and process a few seconds longer. Form into a ball and rest it in the refrigerator overnight.

(con't next page)

CHICKEN PIE (CON'T)

Next day roll half of the crust very thin. Place in bottom and sides of 10" pan.

Bake crust at 400° for 15 minutes and set aside.

Sauté mushrooms, red and green pepper and onion. Set aside. Heat butter and curry and stir in flour. Add chicken stock, heavy cream, salt and pepper. Add mushroom mixture and chicken and simmer for 5 minutes. Let cool. Fill pie pan with mix and roll out remaining dough for top crust. Prick with a fork.

Bake at 400° for 25 minutes.

Ruth Jerge

CHICKEN AND RICE

1 cup cream of celery soup, undiluted

1 cup cream of chicken soup, undiluted

3 whole boned chicken breasts

1 pkg. onion soup mix

1 cup uncooked rice

1 soup can dry white wine

Mix all ingredients except chicken together and chill overnight. Place chicken in a 9"x12" dish. Spread chilled mixture over chicken and cover.

Bake at 325° for 1 hour. Stir and bake for 1 hour longer.

Florence Smith

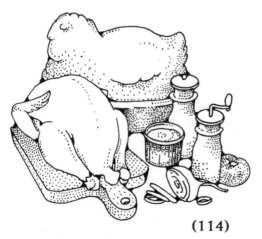

(114)

CHICKEN STIR-FRY

1 cup uncooked rice	4 Tbsp. oil, divided
1 lb. chicken sliced thin	1 large carrot, julienned
3 Tbsp. cornstarch, divided	1 large onion, sliced
4 Tbsp. soy sauce, divided	1 large green pepper,
1 tsp. sugar	cut in strips

Cook rice as directed on package. Combine 2 Tbsp. each, cornstarch and soy sauce with the chicken and sugar. Marinate 30 minutes. Mix remaining cornstarch, soy sauce and 2/3 cup water and set aside. Heat 2 Tbsp. oil in skillet and add chicken and fry 4 minutes. Remove. Heat remaining oil and add carrot, pepper, onion and fry 4 minutes. Stir in chicken mixture. Cook stirring till boils and thickens. Serve over rice.

Sherry Bauer

JOHNNY'S CHICKEN CASSEROLE

1 whole chicken	2 lg. stalks celery, cut up
2 cans cream of mushroom soup	2 eggs
1 pkg. Pepperidge Farm stuffing	Chicken stock
1 onion, chopped	

Cook chicken in water. Cool and remove from bones, saving the stock. Cut chicken in small pieces. In a large greased casserole put half of the chicken. Spread 1 can of soup. Make stuffing with mix, onion and celery. Layer on half of the stuffing mixture, then the rest of the chicken, the other can of soup and the rest of the stuffing. Beat the eggs and pour over casserole.
Bake at 375° for 30 minutes. Good enough for company!

Joan Pearson

GOLD MEDAL CHICKEN

1 3/4 cup stuffing mix	1/4 cup buttermilk
1/4 cup Parmesan cheese	4 chicken breasts
3 Tbsp. butter, melted	

Place stuffing mix in plastic bag. Crush with a rolling pin. Add parmesan cheese to bag and shake well. Place melted butter and buttermilk in a medium bowl and mix well. Dip chicken breasts, one at a time, in milk mixture to coat completely. Place chicken in bag. Close bag and shake well. Place on a baking sheet.
Bake at 350° for 30 minutes. Serves 4.

Elmer Gorham

ONE-DISH GREEK CHICKEN

1 chicken, cut up	Slices of lemon
Potatoes, cut in large cubes	Sliced onions
3 or 4 cloves garlic, minced	Salt & pepper
Oregano	Paprika
Parsley	Melted butter

Put pieces of cut up chicken in casserole. Add the rest of the ingredients pouring the melted butter over all.
Bake at 350° until chicken is done.

Ruth Jerge

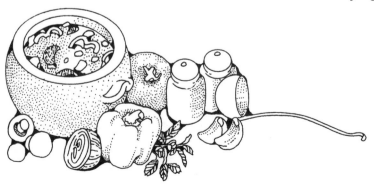

SCALLOPED CHICKEN

1 whole chicken
1 cup flour
4 eggs
1 1/2 qts. prepared
  stuffing (your favorite)

Margarine
Salt
Milk
Bread crumbs

Cook chicken until done, saving broth. Remove from bones and cut up. Let the broth cool and remove fat. Blend 1 cup fat (add margarine to make enough) with the flour and some salt. Beat in eggs. Add enough milk to make 2 quarts of sauce. Cook until smooth. Make your favorite bread dressing and moisten with some of the broth.
Layer 9"x13" pan first with the dressing, then half of the sauce, cover with the chicken and then the rest of the sauce. Butter the bread crumbs and sprinkle on top.
Bake at 350° for 30 to 40 minutes.

Ruth Jerge

SOUTH CAROLINA CHICKEN

2 1/2 - 3lbs. chicken breasts
1 16 oz. jar orange marmalade
1 pkg. onion soup mix

1 16 oz. bottle Russian or
  Catalina dressing

Clean chicken and place pieces in 9"x13" pan. Combine remaining ingredients and pour over chicken.
Bake, covered at 350° for 45 minutes. Remove cover and bake 15 to 25 minutes longer or until chicken is fully cooked.
Great with rice!

Lois Farley

(117)

STIR-FRIED CHICKEN WITH PEANUTS
(For a crowd!)

9 lbs. boned & skinned chicken
   breasts
6 oz. egg whites
1 3/4 oz. cornstarch
1 quart peanut oil
3 cups water chestnuts, drained
3 cups bamboo shoots, drained
18 green onions, cut into pieces
1/3 cup chopped garlic

2 Tbsp. hot pepper paste
1 cup soy sauce
1 cup rice wine
3 Tbsp. sugar
6 Tbsp. vinegar
2 Tbsp. sesame oil
2 Tbsp. water
3/4 cup cornstarch
15 oz. unsalted, roasted
   peanuts

Cut chicken into 1" cubes. Combine with egg whites and 1 3/4oz. cornstarch. Let marinade for 2 hours. Heat peanut oil over high heat until smoking. Reduce heat to medium. Add chicken in 1 lb. batches; cook and stir for 2 minutes. Remove chicken and set aside. Drain off all but 3/4 cup oil. Add water chestnuts, bamboo shoots, green onions, garlic and pepper paste. Cook and stir for 2 minutes. Combine and blend soy sauce, wine, sugar, vinegar, sesame oil, water and 3/4 cup cornstarch. Stir into vegetables. Add cooked chicken. Cook and stir several minutes until sauce slightly thickens. Add peanuts and stir to combine. Serve immediately. 24 servings.

Elmer Gorham

TURKEY LOAF

2 lbs. lean ground turkey breast
1/2 cup fresh bread crumbs
1/2 cup chopped onion
1/2 cup chopped parsley
1/4 cup chopped celery
1/4 cup toasted walnuts

1 Tbsp. marg., softened
3/4 tsp. lemon pepper
1/2 tsp. salt
1 clove minced garlic
4 Tbsp. frozen apple juice,
   thawed and divided

(con't next page)

TURKEY LOAF (CON'T)

Preheat oven to 350°. Coat a 9"x13" baking dish with cooking spray. In a large bowl combine turkey, bread crumbs, onions, parsley, celery, walnuts, margarine, lemon pepper, salt, garlic and 3 Tbsp. apple juice concentrate. Mix well. Shape the mixture into a loaf and place in the prepared pan. Brush the loaf with the remaining apple juice.
Bake 1 1/2 hours or until nicely browned and cooked through. Makes 8 servings.

Virginia Strablow

AUNT CAROL'S SCALLOPED OYSTERS

1 pint oysters   1/3 cup butter
1 cup cracker crumbs   1 cup milk

In a baking dish, layer oysters, cracker crumbs and dot with butter between the layers. Pour milk over the top.
Bake at 350° for 50 to 60 minutes.

Sherry Bauer

CHOPSTICK TUNA

1 can cream of mushroom soup   1 can chowmein noodles
1/4 cup water   1 7 oz. can tuna
1 cup chopped celery   1/2 cup salted cashews
1/4 cup chopped onion   Pepper

Mix water with soup. Add the rest of the ingredients, except only 1/2 can noodles and mix well. Place in an ungreased casserole and sprinkle top with remaining noodles.
Bake at 350° for 15 minutes...no longer! Serves 4.

Florence Smith

(119)

FILET OF SOLE IN LEMON PARSLEY BUTTER
(Microwave)

1/4 cup margarine
1 Tbsp. lemon juice
Salt & pepper to taste
1/2 lb. sole, haddock, etc.

1 Tbsp. flour
1/2 Tbsp. snipped parsley
Dash of celery seed

Melt margarine. Blend in flour and seasonings. Coat both sides of the fish with the sauce.
Cover and microwave on high for 5 to 6 minutes. May be cooked in oven until flaky.

Donna May Barnes

POACHED SALMON

2/3 cup dry white wine
1 1/2 Tbsp. lemon juice
1/2 cup water
1 bay leaf

1 tsp. salt
1/4 tsp. pepper
1 stalk of celery, chopped
3 or 4 salmon steaks or
1-2 lb. salmon fillet

Combine all ingredients except salmon in a large skillet and bring to a boil. Reduce heat and add salmon. Cover and poach at a simmer for 15 minutes or until salmon is opaque and flakes easily when tested with a fork. Remove salmon from liquid with a slotted spoon and place on a warm platter. Decorate with fresh parsley, sliced cucumber, lemon and a little sour cream.

Mary Lou Hallatt

SEAFOOD BISQUE

1 lb. imitation crab flakes
1/2 lb. bite size shrimp
1 can chicken broth
1 large onion
2 stalks celery
1 quart half & half
1 tsp. Worcestershire sauce

1 tsp. black pepper
1 stick butter
1 cup flour
1/8 tsp. ground cloves
Salt as required
Olive oil

Prepare a rue by melting a stick of butter in a sauce pan and slowly stirring in a cup of flour. Do not boil! When butter and flour are mixed thoroughly remove from heat. Chop onion and celery and sauté in olive oil. Add Worcestershire sauce, pepper, cloves and chicken broth. Cook for a few minutes but do not boil. Add shrimp and crabmeat and cook for 5 minutes. Again, do not boil! Add half and half. Thicken by adding rue mixture and cook on low, stirring until thick.

Terry J. Miller

SPICY BAKED FISH FOR TWO

1/2 lb. skinless fillets, fresh
   or frozen
1 Tbsp. chopped onion
1 Tbsp. chopped green pepper

4 oz. canned tomatoes
1/8 tsp. salt
Pinch of pepper
1 tsp. oil

If using frozen, thaw the fish. Grease a small baking pan lightly with 1/4 tsp. oil. Cut the fish into 2 servings. Place them in the baking pan.
Bake at 350° until flaky. Drain the cooking liquid from the fish. While the fish is cooking, cook the onion, green pepper in the remaining oil until the onion is clear. Cut up the large pieces of tomato. Add the tomatoes, salt and pepper to the cooked onion and green pepper. Cook 20 minutes to blend the flavors. Pour the sauce over the drained fish. Bake 10 minutes longer.
Serves two.

Virginia Strablow

RECIPES & NOTES

SIDE DISHES

BARBECUE BEANS

1 can Grandma Browns beans	1/4 cup brown sugar
1 can lima beans	1 Tbsp. dry mustard
1 can kidney beans	1 chopped onion
1/4 cup water	2 Tbsp. vinegar
1 cup catsup	1/2 lb. ground beef

Brown beef and drain. Drain liquid from lima and kidney beans. Mix all of the ingredients together.
Bake at 400° for 1/2 hour.

Patricia O. Few

BEAN BAKE

1 lb. pork sausage	3/4 cup chopped celery
2 cans pork & beans	3/4 cup chopped onion
1 can lima beans, drained	2 Tbsp. prepared mustard
1 can wax beans, drained	1/2 cup brown sugar
1 can green beans, drained	1 can seasoned chili beans
1 can tomato soup, undiluted	Tomato paste

Cook sausage and drain well. Mix all ingredients together. Spread tomato paste over top thinned with a little water.
Bake 350° to 375° for 1 hour.

Virginia Strablow

(122)

GREEN BEANS AND CELERY

1 1/2 lbs. fresh green beans   4 1/2 cups sliced celery
1/4 cup butter or margarine   1/2 tsp. salt
Few twists fresh ground pepper

Wash beans and cut off tips. Cook, covered in 1 inch of boiling water 10-12 minutes or until tender. Drain. Melt butter in large skillet over medium heat. Sauté celery for 10 minutes or until crisp-tender. Add cooked beans to skillet and sprinkle with salt and pepper. Stir and heat for 2 minutes over low heat. Makes 6-8 servings.

Virginia Strablow

ORANGE BEAN BAKE

1 lb.15 oz. can Campbell's pork   3 lb. can Grandma Brown's
   and beans   beans
1/2 cup catsup   3 Tbsp.frozen orange juice
1 cup brown sugar   concentrate, thawed
2 Tbsp. instant minced onion   1 tsp. Worcestershire
3 slices cooked bacon, crisp   sauce
   and crumbled

Mix all ingredients together and bake at 375° for 1 1/4 hours uncovered.

Joyce Bull

BAKED LIMA CASSEROLE

1 lb. dry baby limas
1/4 tsp. soda
1/4 lb. salt pork
1/3 cup brown sugar

3 Tbsp. vinegar
1/3 cup molasses
1/3 cup white sugar

Soak beans overnight in water. In the morning, add soda and boil. Drain off water and rinse well. Cover with boiling water. Add salt pork and boil 5-10 minutes. Add sugars, molasses, vinegar, and salt and pepper if desired.
Bake 4-5 hours in a slow oven (covered) or all day in a crock pot.

Christa Caldwell

BROCCOLI PUFF

1 10oz. pkg. frozen broccoli*
1 can condensed cream of
  mushroom soup
2 oz. sharp processed cheese,
  shredded (1/2 cup)

1/4 cup mayonnaise
1 egg, beaten
1 Tbsp. melted butter
Bread crumbs
1/4 cup milk

Cook broccoli and drain thoroughly. Place in baking dish. Stir together soup and shredded cheese. Gradually add milk, mayonnaise and beaten egg stirring until well blended. Pour over broccoli. Sprinkle with flavored bread crumbs and melted butter. *Slightly cooked equivalent of fresh broccoli may be used!
Bake at 350 for 45 minutes or until set.

Ruth Jerge

PUFFED BROCCOLI-CHEESE CASSEROLE

1 can cream of broccoli soup
1 soup can of milk
1/4 cup flour
1 tsp. dry mustard

1/4 tsp. ground red pepper
2 cups shredded cheddar
4 large eggs, separated
1 pkg. frozen, chopped
    broccoli

Thaw broccoli and squeeze dry. Heat oven to 350°. Lightly grease 7"x11"x1 1/2" pan. Mix soup, milk, flour, mustard, pepper in a 3 quart saucepan until blended. Stir over medium heat until almost boiling. Remove from heat and add cheese. Stir until melted. Stir in room temperature egg yolks and broccoli until blended. Cool slightly. Beat egg whites until stiff peaks form. Fold into broccoli mixture. Pour into prepared pan.
Bake 50 minutes or until top is golden and puffy and knife inserted in center comes out clean. Cool 5 minutes.
Serves 8.

Ann Dumych

CABBAGE STIR-FRY

3 medium potatoes
2 Tbsp. teriyaki sauce
1/2 tsp. cornstarch
1/3 cup chopped onion

1 sm. clove minced garlic
2 Tbsp. cooking oil
3 cups shredded cabbage
1 Tbsp. snipped parsley

Peel potatoes and cut into 1/2" cubes. Cook, covered in boiling, salted water 3 to 5 minutes or until barely tender. Drain well. Combine 2 Tbsp. water, teriyaki sauce and cornstarch and set aside. Cook onion and garlic in hot oil for 1 minute. Add cabbage. Stir-fry for 2 minutes. Add potatoes and stir-fry 2 minutes. Add teriyaki mixture and parsley. Cook one minute.
Makes 6 servings.

Virginia Strablow

SAVORY CHEESE PUFF CASSEROLE

6 oz. pkg. Stovetop Stuffing
8 oz. grated cheddar cheese
3 Tbsp. flour

3 Tbsp. margarine, melted
4 eggs
3 1/2 cups milk

Place stuffing crumbs in a 2 quart buttered casserole. Sprinkle with cheese, then sprinkle flour over cheese. Drizzle melted margarine over flour. Combine eggs, milk and veg. seasoning pkg. from stuffing mix. Pour over crumb and cheese layers. Do not Stir!
Bake, uncovered, at 350° 55-60 minutes.

Lois Farley

CORN CASSEROLE

1 can whole kernel corn,
    drained
1 can creamed corn
1 7oz.pkg. corn muffin mix

1 egg
4 Tbsp. melted margarine
2-3 Tbsp. honey
1 small onion, minced
1 cup sour cream

Combine all ingredients.
Bake at 350° for 35-45 minutes (can be made with nonfat plain yogurt instead of sour cream, and 1 egg white to reduce fat). Makes 1 1/2 quart casserole.

Lois Farley

(Dorothy Bobzin Bennett's)
SWEET-SOUR CUCUMBERS

2 medium cucumbers
1/4 cup sugar
1/2 tsp. salt
1 Tbsp. chopped parsley

1/4 cup water
1/2 cup cider vinegar
1/4 tsp. pepper

Slice cucumbers very thin and blot on paper towels to dry. Combine the rest of the ingredients and pour over cucumbers in a bowl or serving dish. Toss gently and chill several hours.

Donna May Barnes

MAKE AHEAD MASHED POTATOES

6 medium potatoes
3/4 stick margarine
Salt to taste

1/2 cup sour cream
1 egg yolk

Boil and dry mash potatoes. Add the rest of the ingredients and beat with electric mixer, getting out all of the lumps. Mixture will be thick but will thin when baked. Place in greased casserole. May be made day ahead and refrigerated. Bake uncovered at 400° for 30 minutes or until soft and hot (may take longer).

Donna Barnes

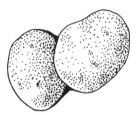

(Sandra Barnes Ranaldi's)
NEW POTATO CASSEROLE

3 Tbsp. minced onion
3 Tbsp. flour
1/4 tsp. paprika
1 cup shredded cheddar cheese
Bread crumbs

5 Tbsp. margarine
1 tsp. salt
1 1/2 cups milk
2 lbs. peeled new potatoes,
  (small size-cooked)
2 Tbsp. melted marg.

Sauté onion in 5 T. margarine. Stir in flour, salt and paprika. Slowly stir in milk to make white sauce. Stir in cheese. Put whole potatoes (about 12 small) in a buttered 1 1/2 quart casserole. Pour cheese sauce over and top with bread crumbs that have been mixed with 2 T. margarine.
Bake at 350° for 20-25 minutes.

Donna May Barnes

PARTY BAKED POTATOES

4 medium baking potatoes, peeled
1/2 cup grated parmesan or Swiss cheese

1/3 cup bread crumbs
1 tsp. salt
6 Tbsp. softened butter

Combine grated cheese, bread crumbs and salt. Cut in butter and mix well. Cut slice from one side of potato to form a flat base. Cut 1/4 inch slices through potato almost to the base but being careful not to cut all the way through. Sprinkle crumb mixture on potatoes.

Bake in a shallow pan at 400° for one hour. Serves 4.

Mary Lou Hallatt

SPUDS A LA ELEGANT

6-8 medium potatoes, (about 2 lbs.) peeled & quartered
1 8 oz. pkg. cream cheese
1 egg, beaten

1/4 tsp. salt
Dash of pepper
1/3 cup minced onion
1/4 cup diced pimento

Cook potatoes in boiling, salted water for 20-25 minutes or until tender. Drain and mash. Add cream cheese, egg, salt and pepper. Beat until smooth. Stir in onion and pimento. If mixture seems dry, stir in 1-2 Tbsp. Milk. Transfer to a buttered 1 1/2 quart casserole.

Bake at 325°, covered, for 40-45 minutes. Serves 6-8.

Laura Shortridge

LADIES CABBAGE

Boil a firm, white cabbage 15 minutes. Change the water and continue boiling until tender. Strain and set aside until cold. Chop fine. Add 2 beaten eggs, 1 Tbsp. butter, 3 Tbsp. milk or cream, salt and pepper and mix.
Bake in a buttered pudding dish until brown. This dish is digestible and palatable, much resembling cauliflower.

SWEET POTATO CASSEROLE

1 can crushed pineapple,
   drained
3 cups canned sweet potatoes
1 cup sugar

1/2 cup milk
1/2 tsp. salt
1 tsp. vanilla
1/3 stick margarine

Topping:
1 cup brown sugar
1 cup coconut
1/2 cup margarine

1 cup nuts
1/2 cup flour

Mash sweet potatoes with the other ingredients. Place in a baking dish. Mix topping ingredients together and sprinkle on top.
Bake at 350° for 35 minutes or microwave on HIGH for 12 minutes.

Gloria J. Wittlinger

SWEET POTATO CASSEROLE

5 lbs. sweet potatoes
3 eggs, beaten
2/3 cup sugar
2/3 cup melted margarine

1/2 cup whipping cream
1 tsp. vanilla
1/2 tsp. nutmeg
1/2 tsp. cinnamon

Topping:
1 cup light brown sugar
1 cup pecans

1/3 cup flour
1/3 cup margarine

Peel, cook and mash sweet potatoes. Mix with the above ingredients (except topping). Place in a casserole. Mix topping ingredients and sprinkle on potato mixture.
Bake at 350° for 60 minutes.

Eileen Dever

ZUCCHINI CASSEROLE

6 cups sliced zucchini	1 cup shredded carrots
1/2 cup chopped onion	1 pkg. herb stuffing mix
1 can cream of chicken soup	1/2 cup melted butter
1 cup sour cream	

Parboil zucchini and onion for 5 minutes in water that has 1/2 tsp. salt added to it. Drain. Combine soup, sour cream and carrots. Fold into zucchini and onions. Combine butter and stuffing mix. Cover bottom of 12"x7"x2" baking pan with half of the stuffing. Spread the zucchini mixture on top. Spread remaining stuffing mixture on top of the zucchini.
Bake at 350° for 30 minutes.

Ann Dumych

POTATO DUMPLINGS
(Kartofel Kloese)

The day before cook a few unpeeled potatoes, but no too soft. Peel them and grate about 2 heaping soup plates full. Put them into a bowl, add a little salt and about 4 to 5 Tbsp. flour. Mix well through the potatoes, then work the yolk of an egg through it all adding in all 3 or 4 eggs. Last, beat the whites to a stiff froth and mix all. Have boiling water ready with a handful of salt in it. Take a spoon and dip it into the water and cut one spoonful after the other into the boiling water. Cook 5 minutes then take out with skimmer. Put on a hot plate and pour browned butter and bread crumbs over all.

RECIPES & NOTES

RECIPES & NOTES

SOUPS, SALADS,

SAUCES

&

DRESSINGS

BROCCOLI-CAULIFLOWER SOUP

1 8 oz. pkg. frozen cauliflower
1 can condensed chicken broth
1 10 oz.pkg. frozen broccoli
1/2 tsp. mustard seed
1/2 tsp. dried dill
1/2 tsp. ground mace

1/3 cup minced onion
1/4 cup butter or marg.
2 Tbsp. flour
1/2 tsp. salt
3 1/2 cups milk
1 cup shredded Swiss cheese

In a 3 quart saucepan cook cauliflower covered in half of the chicken broth for 5 to 8 minutes or just till tender. In a medium saucepan combine remaining chicken broth, broccoli, mustard seed and dill. Cook covered for 5 to 8 minutes until broccoli is just tender. Set aside a few pieces of broccoli for garnish if desired. Remove from heat, cover and keep warm. Place cauliflower mixture and mace in blender or food processor or bowl. Blend or process until smooth. In the 3 qt. saucepan cook onion in butter till tender. Stir in flour, salt and a dash of pepper. Add milk all at once. Cook and stir until thickened and bubbly. Stir sauce, cauliflower mixture and cheese into broccoli mixture. Cook and stir till heated through and cheese is melted. Serves 4 to 6.

Virginia Strablow

HAMBURG SOUP

1 lb. lean ground beef
1 cup diced onion
1 cup cubed raw potato
1 cup cubed raw carrot
1/2 cup diced celery
1 tsp. basil

2 cups canned tomatoes
1 1/2 quarts water
1/4 cup rice or barley
1 small bay leaf
1/2 tsp. thyme

Brown meat well and drain off fat. Add the rest of the ingredients chopping the tomatoes as you add them. Cover and cook over medium heat for 1 hour.

Patricia O. Few

GRANDMA TOMAINO'S ITALIAN SOUP

1 whole soup chicken	2 eggs, beaten
1 lb. ground round	Salt & pepper
1/2 cup grated parmesan cheese	Grated onion, if desired
1 Tbsp. parsley	1/2 cup milk, approx.
1 clove garlic, minced	Acini de pepe macaroni

Make chicken stock using any good stock recipe. Separate chicken from the stock and cut into small pieces. Make small meatballs (about 3/4" thick) using the rest of the ingredients except the small macaroni. Drop meatballs in simmering stock. Remove meatballs when they are cooked through. Cool stock and remove fat. Put stock, meatballs and cut up chicken together. Add the macaroni (about 1 1/2 cups to 6 qts. stock). Cook according to directions on the package. Just before serving, beat 2 eggs and stir into boiling soup.

Serve with parmesan cheese on top.

Note: the 2 eggs and parmesan cheese are in addition to those listed in the ingredients above!

My grandparents were married in Italy in 1901 when grandmother Rosina was only 15 years old. I remember her delicious soup, especially when one of the family was ill, Grandma would always make it for us.

Carolyn Epps

PASTA & BEAN SOUP WITH ESCAROLE

1 Tbsp. olive oil
1 onion, chopped
4 cloves garlic, chopped
1 cup peeled, chopped carrots
1 can (15 oz) cannellini beans, drained

1 can (28 oz) crushed tomatoes
5 cups chicken broth
1/2 cup ditalini macaroni
1 head escarole, coarsely chopped

Heat oil in large soup pot. Add onion, garlic and carrots. Cook on low for 5 minutes or until tender. Add chicken broth and tomatoes and cook for 15 minutes. Add escarole and season with salt and pepper to taste. Cook for 10 minutes. In the meantime cook macaroni in boiling water till tender. Drain pasta and rinse. Add pasta to soup pot. Sprinkle grated cheese on top of each soup bowl when serving. Serves 4.

Elmer Gorham

KAREN BARNES SELLER'S APPLE CELERY MOLD

1 6 oz. pkg. strawberry or lime jello
1 1/2 cups apple juice or cold water
1/4 tsp. cinnamon (optional)

1 cup peeled and diced apple
1/2 cup diced celery
1/4 cup chopped nuts

Dissolve jello in 2 cups boiling water. Add apple juice or water and cinnamon. Chill until thick. Add apple, celery and nuts and pour into a mold and chill until firm.

Donna May Barnes

BEAN SALAD

1 can green beans
1 can yellow beans
1 can kidney beans
1/2 cup chopped or sliced onion

1/2 cup salad oil
1/2 cup vinegar
1/2 cup sugar

Drain green and yellow beans. Rinse kidney beans and drain well. Chick peas may be used in this also. Mix onion, oil, vinegar and sugar until dissolved. Pour over beans and stir lightly. Cover and chill for 12 hours before serving.

Virginia Strablow

ORIENTAL CABBAGE SALAD

1 whole chicken breast,
  cooked and cubed
2 Tbsp. sesame seeds
1/2 cup sliced almonds

1/2 head of shredded
  cabbage
4 green onions, chopped
1 pkg. Ramen noodles

Break up dry noodles and cook as directed, saving the flavoring pkg. for later. Toast sesame seeds and almonds in oven until brown being careful they don't burn. Toss chicken, sesame seeds, almonds, cabbage, onions and noodles together.
Dressing:
1/2 cup salad oil
2 Tbsp. sugar
Noodle flavoring pkg.

1 Tbsp. rice vinegar
1/2 tsp. pepper

Mix all together and pour over salad and mix well. Frozen peas, water chestnuts and celery can be added if desired. Chill overnight.

Ruth Jerge

CHICKEN~ALMOND SALAD

3 cups diced, cooked chicken
1 1/2 cups diced celery
3 Tbsp. lemon juice
1 cup seedless grapes
1 cup toasted almonds
1 cup mayonnaise

3 Tbsp. light cream
1 tsp. dry mustard
1 Tbsp. capers
3/4 tsp. salt
1/8 tsp. pepper

Combine chicken, celery and lemon juice and let stand for 1 hour. Add grapes and almonds and stir. Combine the rest of the ingredients and toss with the chicken mixture. Let stand for 1 hour.
Optional: Use sliced pineapple and mandarin oranges for the grapes and omit the capers.

Anna B. Wallace

HOT CHICKEN SALAD

3 cups diced cooked chicken
2 cans cream of chicken soup
1 cup mayonnaise
4 hard boiled eggs, chopped
2 cans Chinese noodles

2 cups minced celery
4 Tbsp. finely chopped
  onion
Crushed potato chips

Stir soup until smooth. Add mayonnaise then the other ingredients except noodles and chips. Top with the crushed potato chips.
Bake at 350° for 25 to 30 minutes. Serve over Chinese noodles. Serves 6. This could also be used as an entree casserole.

Estelle Dunlap

CONGEALED SALAD

1 box lime jello
1 box lemon jello

1 8 oz. pkg. cream cheese
1 small can crushed
pineapple

Pour jellos together in bowl. Add 2 cups boiling water and stir until dissolved. Chill until soft-set, about 2 hours. In a large mixing bowl blend softened cream cheese and pineapple with the juice. Add the soft-set jello and Stir until well mixed. Pour into jello mold or small casserole dish and chill until firm.
Note: Cherry jello may also be used in place of the lemon and lime.

Laura Shortridge

FRUIT AND MACARONI SALAD

1 lb. Rosa Marina macaroni
2 cans pineapple chunks
1 bottle maraschino cherries,
  cut up
1 large can mandarin oranges,
  cut up

1 10 oz. cool whip
3/4 cup sugar
2 eggs
3 Tbsp. flour

Cook macaroni and drain. Drain juice from pineapple and oranges and save. Beat eggs, add sugar and flour mixture. Add the juice. Cook over medium heat until thickened. Add to macaroni and let stand overnight. Add cut up fruit to macaroni and fold in cool whip.

Virginia Strablow

FRUIT SALAD

1 lg. can fruit cocktail, drained
1 can chunk pineapple, drained
2 cans mandarin oranges, drained
1 cup maraschino cherries, cut in half & drained
3/4 cup sugar
Pinch of salt
1 1/2 cups mini marshmallows
1/2 to 3/4 cup Rosa Marina macaroni
1 medium Cool Whip
2 eggs
3 Tbsp. flour

Cook macaroni according to directions, drain and cool. Cook juices from canned fruit with beaten eggs, sugar, flour and salt. When cool fold thickened juices with macaroni and chill overnight. About 2 hours before serving, mix the fruit and marshmallows with the thickened juices and macaroni. Seedless grapes and sliced banana may be added at this time also if desired.

Ruth Jerge

GELATIN COTTAGE CHEESE SALAD

1 lb. cottage cheese
1 pkg. orange jello
1 small container Cool Whip
1 small can mandarin oranges, drained

Stir jello powder into the cottage cheese. Add the oranges and Cool Whip. Chill and serve. You can use any drained fruit or different flavors of jello.

Virginia Strablow

PASTA SALAD YOLANDA

1 8 oz. pkg. cooked pasta
1 cucumber, cut in pieces
1 cup chopped celery
1 fresh tomato, cut up
1 red bell pepper
1/2 cup fresh basil
1 cup Italian dressing
1 cup Parmesan cheese

Mix together and serve.

Yolanda Gilchrist

LEMON~LIME HORSERADISH SALAD

1 pkg. lemon gelatin
1 pkg. lime gelatin
2 cups boiling water
1 #2 can crushed pineapple
1 cup evaporated milk or
  dairy sour cream

1 cup small curd cottage
  cheese
1/2 cup chopped pecans,
  (optional)
1/2 cup salad dressing
2 Tbsp. grated horseradish

Dissolve gelatins in boiling water and add pineapple with juice. Chill until partially set. Mix the rest of the ingredients and fold into the gelatin. Pour into a mold and chill overnight.
NOTE: If using a ring mold, take 2 Tbsp. gelatin and mix with 2 Tbsp. water for top "decoration" to fill the indentation.

Anna B. Wallace

PINEAPPLE GELATIN SALAD

1 3oz. pkg. lemon gelatin
1 cup boiling water
1 20oz. can crushed pineapple
  and juice
10 large marshmallows, cut in
  small pieces

1/2 lb. mashed cottage
  cheese
1 or 2 cups Cool Whip
1/2 cup chopped nuts
8~10 slivered maraschino
  cherries

Mix gelatin with boiling water and add pineapple and juice and marshmallows. Cool. When slightly thickened, add the rest of the ingredients. Pour into a pan and refrigerate overnight.

Anna B. Wallace

POTATO SALAD

5 lbs. potatoes (white or red),
  cooked
1 red onion, diced

1 lb. green beans, boiled

1 jar poppy seed dressing
  (con't next page)

(138)

POTATO SALAD (CON'T)

The following items can be used to season to taste: salt, pepper and/or dill weed. Wash potatoes and boil. Peel them if you wish and dice. Toss together, chill & serve.

Yolanda Gilchrist

GERMAN POTATO SALAD

6 slices bacon
6-8 medium potatoes
1 medium onion
1/2 cup sugar
2 heaping Tbsp. cornstarch

1/2 cup cider vinegar
1 tsp. salt
Pepper to taste
1 3/4 cups water

Cook potatoes and peel. Slice into a bowl. Cook bacon and drain on paper towel. Stir cornstarch into bacon grease. Add salt, vinegar, onion, seasonings and water. Boil and stir until thick. Pour over potatoes. Let stand to soak up the sauce. A little green pepper cut up fine and whole celery seeds make a good addition also. Stir in crisp bacon before serving.

Ruth Jerge

GERMAN POTATO SALAD

6 potatoes
1 large onion or 6 green
  onions chopped
1 stalk celery
6-8 slices bacon
3 eggs

1/3 cup water
1/3 cup sugar
1/2 cup vinegar
1 tsp. celery seed
1/4 tsp. paprika
Salt & pepper to taste

Cook potatoes, peel and slice them. Slice celery and onions. Fry bacon until crisp and remove from pan. Add the water to the bacon grease. Then add beaten eggs, sugar, celery seed, salt and pepper. Cook until it starts to boil. Pour over the potatoes. Sprinkle crumbled bacon over top. Serve warm.

Alma Miller

(139)

SHRIMP ASPIC SALAD

1 pkg. lemon jello
1 Tbsp. vinegar
1 cup boiling water
1 Tbsp. horseradish
3/4 cup tomato juice

1/4 cup diced celery
1/4 cup peas
1 tsp. grated onion
1 can cleaned shrimp

Dissolve jello in boiling water. Add tomato juice, vinegar and horseradish. Cool slightly. Add rest of ingredients. Pour into a mold and chill until firm.

Eunice Hernberger

LAYERED SPINACH SALAD

1 bag washed spinach,
   torn up
1 pkg. frozen peas, thawed
1 can sliced water chestnuts
1 pkg. sliced mushrooms
1 red onion, chopped

3 hardboiled eggs, cut up
5 slices bacon
3/4 cup Parmesan cheese
1 1/2 cups mayonnaise
1 1/2 cups sour cream
3 Tbsp. sugar

Cook bacon, drain, crumble and set aside. Dressing: Mix mayonnaise, sour cream and sugar and set a side.
Layer 1: Half of the spinach, eggs and small amount of dressing
Layer 2: Peas, onions, mushrooms and more dressing
Layer 3: Rest of the spinach, water chestnuts, bacon, cheese and the rest of the dressing.
Refrigerate overnight. Can be served in layers or tossed!

Maggie Lupo

(140)

AUNT SUSIE'S RAW VEGETABLE SALAD

2 cups raw cauliflower
2 cups raw broccoli
2 cups raw carrots
1/2 cup mayonnaise or Miracle
  Whip

1/4 cup milk
1/4 or less brown sugar
1 Tbsp. vinegar

Cut up raw vegetables. Mix the rest of the ingredients together and pour over the vegetables. You can add chopped celery or green peppers if you have them and like them in a vegetable dish.

Sherry Bauer

WALDORF CROWN SALAD

2 3 oz. pkgs. strawberry jello
2 cups boiling water
1 1/2 cups cold water
1 cup cubed apples
1/2 cup thin sliced celery

1/4 cup chopped walnuts
1 cup dairy sour cream
1/2 cup salad dressing
1 1/2 cups miniature
  marshmallows

Combine sour cream and salad dressing. Fold in marshmallows and set aside. Dissolve jello in boiling water and stir in cold water. Chill until thickened. Fold in apples, celery and nuts. Pour into a 5 cup ring mold. Chill until firm. Unmold. Surround with lettuce. Fill center with dressing and garnish with apple slices and walnut half if desired.

Arvilla Hall

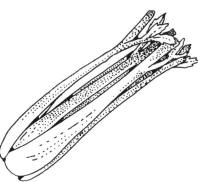

WILTED LETTUCE

1 large head leaf lettuce
4 slices bacon
4-6 green onions with tops

3 Tbsp. vinegar
2 tsp. vinegar

Break lettuce into pieces in bowl and sprinkle with salt and pepper. Fry bacon until crisp. Drain, crumble and add to lettuce. Add remaining ingredients to bacon fat in pan. Bring to a boil and pour over lettuce. Toss lightly until wilted.

> **CHILI SAUCE**
> *Chop 18 ripe tomatoes, 3 onions, 2 green peppers. Mix with 2 1/2 cups vinegar, 1 cup sugar, 1 tsp. cloves, 1 tsp. cinnamon and 2 tsp. salt. Boil down slowly. Seal in jars.*

Estelle Dunlap

AMARETTO SAUCE

1 pkg. instant vanilla pudding
1 cup milk

1/2 cup amaretto
1 small Cool Whip

Beat pudding mix, milk and amaretto until thick. Fold in Cool Whip.
Wonderful on fruit salad!

Christa Caldwell

LEMON SAUCE

1 cup sugar
1/4 tsp. salt
2 Tbsp. cornstarch
1 cup juice from fresh lemons

4 cups boiling water
1 Tbsp. butter
2 Tbsp. lemon rind

Mix sugar, salt and cornstarch in pan. Add rest of the ingredients and cook until thickened.

Patricia O. Few

MUSTARD SAUCE

1/2 cup sugar	1 egg
2 tsp. dry mustard	1/4 cup milk
1/2 tsp. salt	1/4 cup vinegar

Mix dry ingredients thoroughly. Stir in egg and add milk and vinegar. Bring just to a boil (but do not boil) stirring constantly. The sauce will thicken on cooling.

This sauce is great over ham. A few dry currents or raisins may be added if desired.

Patricia O. Few

UNCOOKED CHILI SAUCE

8 qts. tomatoes	1 qt. cider vinegar
1 cup salt	2 oz. mustard seed
6 cups or less sugar	3 medium onions, chopped
1 cup grated horseradish	3 chopped hot peppers
2 bunches diced celery	3 diced green peppers

Peel tomatoes and chop fine. Add salt. Mix well. Let stand overnight. In the morning drain dry and add remaining ingredients making sure sugar is dissolved. Pour into sterilized jars. Affix lids and process in boiling water bath for 5 minutes.

Using this method most of the salt drains out of the tomatoes.

Betty Roadarmel

FRENCH DRESSING

1/2 cup oil	1 tsp. lemon juice
1/4 cup vinegar	1 tsp. salt
1/3 cup catsup	1/3 cup sugar

Put all ingredients in a blender. Run until thick.

Joyce Bull

(143)

GOOD-FOR-YOU SALAD DRESSING

1 cup low salt tomato juice	1 tsp. prepared mustard
1/4 cup vinegar	2 tsp. onion flakes
1 1/2 tsp. Worcestershire sauce	Dash of cinnamon
	Dash garlic powder (opt)
1/2 pkg. sugar substitute	2 tsp. low-salt chicken bouillon crystals

Mix well together. If desired, add 2 Tbsp. oil.

Christa Caldwell

TOMATO GRAVY

Tomatoes	Margarine
Milk	Flour
Sugar	Salt & Pepper

In an iron skillet, cook quartered tomatoes in margarine. Remove skins and simmer until "caramelized". Add milk and enough flour and water mixed together to the consistency that you like when cooked. Season with salt and pepper and a touch of sugar.
Serve on buttered toast for breakfast, lunch or supper!

Mary Newhard

RECIPES & NOTES

RECIPES & NOTES

CANNING

&

MISCELLANEOUS

UNCOOKED CHILI SAUCE
(See Sauces p. 144)

BREAD AND BUTTER PICKLES

6 cucumbers
1 red pepper
1 green pepper
4 cups ice water
1/2 cup salt

2 cups vinegar
2 cups boiling water
1 Tbsp. mustard seed
1 1/2 cups sugar

Thinly slice vegetables. Combine ice water, salt and vegetables. Let stand 2 hours and drain. Combine vinegar, sugar, boiling water and spices. Bring to a boil and add vegetables. Simmer until tender. Put in jars, cover with syrup and seal.

Betty Roadarmel

HORSERADISH PICKLES

1 1/2 qts. dill pickles*
1/3 cup water
4 oz. horseradish

1 1/2 cups sugar
2/3 cup vinegar

Drain the pickles (*use no garlic Polish dills). Cut lengthwise or into chunks. make a brine of the sugar, vinegar and water and bring to a boil. Add the horseradish and pour over the pickles. Let them stand in the refrigerator for 5 days, turning the jar over 2 or 3 times a day. You can reuse the brine one more time.

Jim Langton

REDONE DILL PICKLES

1 qt. commercial dill pickles
12 whole cloves or
  1 Tbsp. pickling spices

1 stick cinnamon
1 3/4 cup sugar

Drain the pickles and slice medium thick in a large bowl. Sprinkle over them the cinnamon broken into small pieces, cloves and sugar. Don't stir. Let stand at room temperature, covered for 24 hours.
2nd day: Stir slowly a few times, every now and then.
3rd day: Put pickles back in the jar and replace the cover. Store in the refrigerator.

Anna B. Wallace

RHUBARB CONSERVE

5 cups rhubarb, finely cut
5 cups sugar

1 can crushed pineapple
2 pkgs. strawberry jello

Boil rhubarb, sugar and pineapple with juice for 20 minutes. Add the jello powder. Bring back to a boil and bottle.

Esther Casselman

HOLIDAY MARMALADE

1 fresh pineapple
2 oranges
2 lemons
1/2 cup shredded coconut

5 cups sugar
1 12oz.pkg. frozen tart red
  cherries

Core, peel and finely chop pineapple and put in large saucepan. Seed oranges and lemons and put through grinder with course blade. Add to pineapple. Add sugar and bring mixture to a boil, stirring until sugar is dissolved. Cook rapidly to 220°, about 40 minutes. Add cherries and coconut and cook 10 minutes. Carefully ladle hot marmalade into stirile jars, leaving 1/4 inch headspace. Wipe jars clean. Replace jar lids evenly but firmly. Do not use excessive force. Process 10 minutes in a boiling water canner.

Good Neighbor,
Dave Marmon

PRUNE CONSERVE

4 lbs. prunes (approx. 55)
2 oranges
Sugar

Juice of 1 lemon
1/2 lb. walnut pieces

Wash prunes, pit and cut into small pieces. Thinly slice oranges and then cut into small pieces and add to prunes. Measure and add 3/4 cup sugar to each cup of cut up fruit. Cook until thick like jam. Stir to keep from sticking. Add lemon juice and nuts and stir to heat the nuts. Seal in sterile jars.
This was my Great-Grandma Thorn's recipe!

Melissa Dunlap

SPICED PEACHES

1/2 bushel peaches, peeled
4 cups vinegar
8 cups sugar

2 Tbsp. whole cloves
3 sticks cinn. (broken)

Mix ingredients except peaches in kettle. Cook until clear. Add peaches enough for one jar at a time and cook 3-5 minutes or until tender. Jar and seal adding more syrup if necessary.
NOTE: If the peaches are small, use whole peaches, including the pit. If the peaches are larger, halve the peaches and include 2 pits in the jar for quarts and 1 pit for pints.

Estelle Dunlap

SHAKE AND BAKE

1 cup flour or 1/2 cup flour &
   1/2 cup cornmeal
1/4 tsp. pepper

1/2 tsp. celery powder
1 tsp. paprika
2 tsp. salt (if desired)

Mix together and keep ready to use for meats.

Sherry Bauer

STUFFING SEASONING MIX

1 tsp. poultry seasoning
1 tsp. chicken bouillon
1 Tbsp. dried celery

2 tsp. dried onion
2 tsp. parsley, crushed

Package in an air tight container until ready to use.

(con't next page)

STUFFING SEASONING MIX (CON'T)

When ready to use:

1 1/4 cups water	4 cups bread cubes
3 Tbsp. margarine	Seasoning mix

Combine water, margarine and seasoning mix. Bring to a boil and reduce to simmer. Simmer 5 minutes. Stir in bread cubes, cover and remove from heat. Let stand 5 minutes.

Sherry Bauer

ELEPHANT STEW

1 elephant	Salt & pepper to taste
2 rabbits (optional)	

Cut elephant into bite size pieces. This should take about two months. Add enough brown gravy to cover. Cook over kerosene fire for 4 weeks at 465°. This will serve 3,800 people. If more are expected, 2 rabbits may be added, but do so only if necessary, as most people do not like hare in their stew!

Christa Caldwell
Virginia Strablow

HOW TO COOK A HUSBAND

A good many husbands are entirely spoiled by mismanagement in cooking, and so are not tender and good. Some women keep them too constantly in hot water; others freeze them; others put them in a stew; others keep them eternally in a pickle. It cannot be supposed that any husband will be good and tender if managed in this way, but they are truly delicious if properly treated.

Don't keep him in the kettle by force, as he will stay there himself if proper care is taken; if he should sputter and fizz, don't be anxious...some husbands do this. Add a little sugar, the variety that confectioners call "kisses", but on no account add vinegar or pepper! A little spice improves him, but it must be used with judgement. Do not try him with something sharp to see if he is tender. Stir him gently lest he lie too long in the kettle and become flat and tasteless.

If you follow these directions, you will find him very digestible, agreeing nicely with you, and he will keep as long as you want to have him!

Christa Caldwell

RECIPES & NOTES

RECIPES & NOTES

SPECIAL

HERITAGE

SECTION

BUTTERMILK PANCAKES

3 eggs
1 Tbsp. baking soda
1 Tbsp. baking powder

1 tsp. salt
1 quart buttermilk
3 cups unbleached flour

Mix eggs until light and fluffy. Add buttermilk and mix. Then add baking powder, baking soda, salt and mix. Add flour and mix. Should be a thin mixture. You might have to add a little milk. The pancakes should be 1/4 inch thick on the griddle.
NOTE: For a lower fat pancake use 6 egg whites instead of the 3 eggs and use a low-fat buttermilk!
This recipe has been used by the Linnabery family for 150 years!

Miles Linnabery

CORN BREAD

1 cup flour
3 tsp. baking powder
1/2 tsp. salt
1/2 cup sugar

1/2 cup yellow corn meal
1 cup milk
1 egg, well beaten
1 Tbsp. melted shortening

Mix and sift flour, baking powder, salt and sugar. Stir in corn meal. Add milk, beaten egg and stir into the first mixture. Add shortening. Blend and turn into pan (use a heavy iron skillet, heavily greased and heated for 5 minutes).
Bake at 400° for 20 minutes. Cut into 6 squares. Serve hot. Very good with honey.

Betty Allen
Taken from Niagara Falls DAR Heritage Recipes-1990
with permission - Compiled by Ann Bruski

DATE BREAD

1 6oz. box dates, cut up
1 Tbsp. shortening
1 cup light brown sugar
1 egg

2 2/3 cups flour
2 tsp. baking soda
1 tsp. vanilla
1/2 tsp. salt

Let dates stand in 1 1/2 cups boiling water to cook until soft.   Mix all ingredients together and put in 3 tin cans (corn or pea size).
Bake at 350° for 1 hour.   Cut bottom out of can and slip out. Slice and serve.

Ann Bruski

DATE BREAD

1 cup dates, cut fine
1 Tbsp. butter
1 egg
1 1/2 cups flour

1 cup boiling water
1/2 cup sugar
1 tsp. baking soda

Pour boiling water on dates and let cool. Sift soda and flour together.   Cream butter and add sugar.   Add beaten egg. Alternately add the dry ingredients and date mixture.
Bake at 375° for 2 small loaves for approximately 35 minutes.
Bake at 350° for 1 large loaf for 1 hour.

Esther Prudden
Taken from Niagara Falls DAR Heritage Recipes-1990
with permission ~ compiled by Ann Bruski

FOUNDATION SWEET DOUGH
(Basic dough-Mennonite Cook Book Version)

1 cup scalded milk	1 1/2 tsp. salt
1 cup lukewarm water	2 eggs, beaten
2 cakes compressed yeast	7 cups flour
1/2 cup shortening	1/2 tsp. nutmeg or 1/2
1/2 cup sugar	lemon rind & juice

Pour scalded milk over sugar, salt and shortening. Dissolve yeast in lukewarm water and add beaten eggs. When milk has cooled has cooled to lukewarm add the yeast egg mixture. Beat well. Add flour and seasonings gradually, beating well. Knead lightly, working in just enough flour so that dough can be handled. Place dough in greased bowl, cover and let stand in a warm place. Let rise until double in bulk (about 2 hours). Make into cinnamon, butterscotch or pecan rolls (let rolls rise).
Bake at 400° about 25 minutes.

Olive Burch
Taken from Niagara Falls DAR Heritage Recipes-1990
with permission-compiled by Ann Bruski

JOHNNY CAKE

3 Tbsp. butter	1 cup cornmeal
1/2 cup sugar	1 cup flour
1 egg	1 tsp. baking soda
1 cup sour milk	

Cream butter the size of an egg (approx. 3 Tbsp.) and sugar. Add egg and stir. Add sour milk, corn meal, flour and baking soda. Mix well. Pour into a square greased pan.
Bake at 375° for 25-30 minutes.
Inez notes: This is a very old recipe from the early 1900's and is a bread not a cake!

Inez Metz
Patricia O. Few

HARDTACK

Also known as 'tack, ironplate biscuits, army bread, etc.'. Found in the "1862 US Army Book of Receipts", this is one recipe that is guaranteed to keep your dentist happy with bridge and upper plate work. A square biscuit made of flour and water, it was the mainstay of soldiers North and South during the War Between the States and the forerunner of the saltines we know today. Although its hardness made it last forever, it made it almost impossible to eat. A sign in the museum in Manassas asserts that it is no harder today than it was when it came out of the oven 135 years ago.

Hardtack was generally broken up with a rock or rifle butt, placed in the cheek and softened with saliva until it could be chewed. It could also be soaked in water and then fried in bacon grease to produce a concoction known as "coosh".

The receipt (recipe) follows:

5 cups flour	1 1/4 cups water
1 Tbsp. baking powder	1 Tbsp. salt

Preheat oven to 450°. In a bowl, combine the ingredients to form a stiff, but not dry dough. The dough should be pliable, but not stick a lot to your hands. Flatten out dough onto a greased cookie sheet (the ones with a small lip around the edge) and roll the dough into a flat sheet 1/2 inch thick.

Using a bread knife, divide the dough into 3"x3" squares. Taking a 10-penny nail, put a matrix of holes into the surface of the dough, all the way through, at even intervals. Bake for approx. 20 minutes until light brown. Take out and let cool.

NOTE: Do this the day before you go on the field and you will have enough tack to fill your haversack. It will be somewhat soft on Saturday morning, but, by Sunday, you should soak it in your coffee before eating.

Tim Kirsch,
NCHS Explorer Post #128
of the 28th NYVI

SODA BREAD
from *The Book of Household Management* (1862)

Ingredients: To every 2 lbs. of flour allow 1 tsp. tartaric acid, 1 tsp. salt, 1 tsp. carbonate of soda and 2 breakfast-cupfuls of cold milk.

Mode: Let the tartaric acid and salt be reduced to the finest possible powder, then mix them well with the flour. Dissolve the soda in the milk and pour it several times from one basin to another, before adding it to the flour. Work the whole quickly into a light dough, divide it into 2 loaves and put them into a well-heated oven immediately.
Bake for 1 hour. Sour milk or buttermilk may be used, but then a little less acid will be needed.

Modern Conversion

7~8 cups flour   1 tsp. cream of tartar
2 cups cold milk   1 tsp. salt
1 tsp. baking soda

Mix flour, cream of tartar and salt together. Dissolve the baking soda in the milk. Add milk to the flour. Stir the mixture into a ball and divide in two.
Bake in a preheated oven at 350° for 45~60 minutes on a greased tray or pan.

Compliments of Dundern Castle
Hamilton, Ontario, Canada

FIG FILLING FOR SANDWICHES
from the *Larkin Housewives' Cook Book* 4th edition

6 preserved figs   Raspberry jam
1/2 cup walnuts   Butter
Brown bread

Chop the figs and walnuts fine and mix with enough raspberry jam to spread well. Butter thin slices of brown bread and spread with the filling. Cut the slices into quarters.

Nancy Piatkowski
Documentary Heritage Program
Buffalo, NY

CIDER CAKE
from *The Frugal Housewife's Manual* (1840)

Take 2 pounds of flour, 1 pound of sugar, 1/2 pound of butter, 1 pint of cider, cloves and cinnamon, with or without fruit, two tsp. saleratus; put the saleratus in the cider and mix it while foaming.
Bake. As a general rule everything mixed with saleratus should be put in the oven immediately.

Modern Conversion

7-8 cups flour   2 cups brown sugar
1/2 lb. butter   1 tsp. cloves and cinnamon
1 1/2 cups cider   Raisins or currents, opt.
2 tsp. baking soda

Dissolve soda in cider and mix while foaming. Mix butter and brown sugar. Add spices and alternately the flour and cider mixture.
Bake at 350° for 45-60 minutes.

Compliments of Dundern Castle,
Hamilton, Ontario, Canada

BLACK CAKE OR PLUM CAKE
from *Seventy-Five Receipts for Pastry, Cakes and Sweetmeats* 1828

One pound of flour, sifted. One pound of fresh butter. One pound of powdered white sugar. Twelve eggs. Two pounds of the best raisins. Two pounds of currents. Two Tbsp. of mixed spice, mace and cinnamon. Two nutmegs, powdered. A large glass of wine and a large glass of brandy mixed together. Half a glass of rose-water. A pound of citron.

Pick the currents very clean, and wash them, draining them through a cullender. Wipe them in a towel. Spread them out on a large dish and set them near the fire or in the hot sun to dry, placing the dish in a slanting position. Having stoned the raisins, cut them in half and when all done, sprinkle them well with sifted flour to prevent their sinking to the bottom of the cake. When currents are dry, sprinkle them also with flour.

Pound the spice, allowing twice as much cinnamon as mace. Sift it, and mix the mace, nutmeg, and cinnamon together. Mix also the liquor and rose-water in a tumbler or cup. Cut the citron in slips. Sift the flour into a broad dish. Sift the sugar into a deep earthen pan and cut the butter into it. Warm it near the fire, if the weather is too cold for it to mix easily. Stir the butter and sugar to a cream.

Beat the eggs as light as possible. Stir them into the butter and sugar alternately with the flour. Stir very hard. Gradually add the spice and liquor. Stir the raisins and currents into the mixture taking care that they are well floured. Stir the whole as hard as possible for ten minutes after all the ingredients are in.

Cover the bottom and sides of a large tin or earthen pan with sheets of white paper, well buttered and put into it some of the mixture. Then spread on it some of the citron which must not be cut too small. Next put a layer of the mixture and then a layer of citron and so on till it is all in, having a layer of the mixture at the top.

This cake is always best baked in a baker's oven and will require four or five hours in proportion to its thickness. Ice it, next day.   (Editorial: WHEW!!!)

(Con't next page)

BLACK CAKE OR PLUM CAKE (con't)
Modern Conversion

2 cups flour

2 cups white sugar

2 cups raisins

4 Tbsp. red wine

2 Tbsp. nutmeg

2 cups candied peel or citron

1 cup butter

12 medium eggs

2 cups dried currents

4 Tbsp. brandy

1 Tbsp. rosewater

2 Tbsp. mixed spice,
(cinnamon and mace)

In a large bowl, mix together all fruit and sprinkle with flour to prevent the fruit from sinking to the bottom of the cake. In a second large bowl, cream butter and sugar. Add spices. Beat the eggs until foaming. Stir in butter, alternating with the flour. Add the fruit and continue mixing for 10 minutes. Line the bottom and sides of your pans with buttered paper.

Bake at 350° for 1 to 1 1/2 hours depending on the size of the pans. Place a container of water in the oven as well to keep the cake moist. When completely cool, ice and decorate as desired.

Compliments of Dundern Castle,
Hamilton, Ontario, Canada

FARMER'S SPONGE CAKE
from *The Canadian Settler's Guide* 1855

One teaspoonful of carbonate of soda dissolved in a tea cupful of sweet milk, two teaspoonfuls of cream of tartar, mixed dry into the flour, one egg, one cup of soft sugar, one cup of butter, melted; it can be made richer by the addition of a cup of currents or spice to flavour it. Mix to a thickish batter, and pour into a flat pan or bake in tins.

Modern Conversion

1 tsp. baking soda	1 cup milk
2 tsp. cream of tartar	2 cups flour
1 egg	1 cup brown sugar
1 cup melted butter	

Dissolve baking soda in milk. In a large bowl mix flour, brown sugar and cream of tartar. Make a well in the middle and add milk, egg and melted butter. This will foam and make a liquid batter.
Bake at 350° in a greased pan for 45 minutes.

Compliments of Dundern Castle,
Hamilton, Ontario, Canada

1863 FRUIT CAKE

2 cups brown sugar
1/2 cup butter*
1/2 cup lard
2 eggs
1 cup buttermilk or sour milk
1 cup raisins, dried apples, prunes,
  or other dried fruit

1 tsp. cinnamon
1 tsp. nutmeg
1/2 tsp. salt
1 tsp. soda
4 cups flour

Cream shortening, sugar and eggs, then beat. Add remaining ingredients. Mix well to soften batter.
Bake at 325° in 2 greased pans 8"x4"x3" until broom straw comes out clean, about 1 1/2 hours. If home dried fruit is used, soak in warm water until soft. Fruitcake stored in a 3~gallon stone jar will keep moist. Yield: 2 loaves.
Note: Check at 1 hour, adjust time to your oven as ovens do vary. * All margarine may be used for the butter and lard! Recipe came from Iowa years ago to me.

Joan Crea

GRANDMOTHER BALCOM'S NEW YEAR'S CAKE

1 cup chopped dates
1 cup boiling water
1/2 cup butter
1 egg
1 cup white sugar
6 Tbsp. melted butter
4 Tbsp. cream

1 tsp. vanilla
1 2/3 cup flour
1 tsp. soda
1/2 tsp. baking powder
1/2 cup chopped nuts
10 Tbsp. brown sugar
1/2 tsp. vanilla

Combine dates and boiling water. Bring back to a boil and then let cool. Set aside. Cream butter, egg, sugar and 1 tsp. vanilla and add to the cooled dates. Add the rest of the ingredients and beat thoroughly. Put in cake pan.
Bake at 350° for 35~40 minutes. Cool cake about 5 minutes.
Combine melted butter, brown sugar, cream and 1/2 tsp. vanilla. Mix and pour on cake carefully. Brown under broiler.

Esther Casselman

KNOBBY APPLE CAKE

2 cups chopped apples
1 cup sugar
1 egg
1/4 cup melted shortening
1 tsp. vanilla
Whipped cream

1 tsp. soda
1 tsp. cinnamon
1/2 cup raisins
1/2 tsp. salt
1/2 cup chopped nuts

Mix apples and sugar together and let stand for 5 minutes.
Mix egg, shortening and vanilla together. Add the rest of
the ingredients, apples last.
Bake at 350° for 40 minutes. Serve warm with whipped
cream.

Beth Bodie
Taken from Niagara Falls DAR Heritage Recipes-1990
with permission-compiled by Ann Bruski

LAURA'S GINGERBREAD
Laura Ingalls Wilder was famous far and wide for
her gingerbread. This was her own recipe!

1 cup brown sugar
½ cup lard or other shortening
1 cup molasses
2 tsp. baking soda
1 cup boiling water
3 cups flour
1 tsp. ginger

1 tsp. cinnamon
1 tsp. allspice
1 tsp. nutmeg
1 tsp. cloves
½ tsp. salt
2 eggs, well beaten

Blend brown sugar with lard. Mix molasses well with
baking soda and water. Do this over your bowl as the
mixture will foam up. Mix well with the first mixture. Sift
salt and spices into the flour and mix into the other
mixture. Lastly, add the eggs. The mixture should be quite
thin. Pour into 9"x13" pan.
Bake at 350° for 30 minutes. Excellent!

Esther Casselman

PORTUGAL CAKES
from *The Art of Cooking Made Plain and Easy*
courtesy of Culinary Historians of Ontario

Mix into a pound of fine flour a pound of loaf sugar beat and sifted, then rub it into a pound of pure sweet butter till it is thick like grated white bread, then put to it two spoonfuls of rosewater, two of sack, 10 eggs, whip them very well with a whisk, then mix into it 8 ounces of currents, mixed all well together; butter the tin pans, fill them but half full and bake them.

Modern Conversion

3 1/2-4 cups white flour
2 cups sweet butter, softened
2 Tbsp. rosewater
1 cup currents, plumped in hot water

2 cups white sugar
10 medium eggs, separated
2 Tbsp. red wine or sherry

Sift flour and sugar together. Rub soft butter in "till it is thick like grated white bread". Add drained currents; whisk egg yolks and wine to a thick cream, about 10 minutes with a wire whisk or 5 minutes with an electric beater. Blend yolks into flour and butter mixture. Whisk whites and rosewater until stiff, about 10 minutes with a wire whisk or 5 minutes with an electric beater. Fold about a quarter of whites into batter to lighten it, then fold in remaining whites. Turn batter into a buttered or greased 9"x13" pan.

Bake at 350° for about 1 hour or until toothpick inserted in center comes out clean.

Compliments of Dundern Castle,
Hamilton, Ontario, Canada

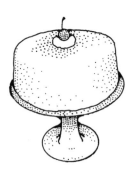

(162)

CHRISTMAS OR WEDDING CAKE

1 lb. butter
1 lb. brown sugar
10 eggs
6 cups flour
1 tsp. soda
1 tsp. ginger
1 Tbsp. cloves
1 Tbsp. nutmeg
1 cup fruit juice

2 Tbsp. cinnamon
1 pt. blackberry jam or
  molasses
2 lbs. almonds
1 lb. citron
1 lb. dates
1 lb. figs
3 lbs. raisins

The day before baking, prepare the fruit, shell and blanch the almonds. The next morning, beat the butter and sugar to a cream, add yolks of eggs beaten light. Then stir the soda into the molasses or jam and add to mixture. Then add flour and spices sifted together and the fruit juice. Dredge the fruit well with flour and add to the mixture, then the almonds and fold in last the whites of eggs beaten to a stiff froth. Line the pan with heavy well-greased paper. Have the citron sliced very thin, put a layer on cake batter, then a layer of citron, alternately until all is used. This cake fills a pan 10 inches in diameter and 5 inches deep.
Bake in a very moderate oven for 6 or 7 hours. This is a splendid cake and will keep for months.

Nancy Piatkowski
Documentary Heritage Program
Buffalo, NY

(163)

PENNSYLVANIA FRUIT CAKE

2/3 cup lard or butter
1 cup sugar
2 eggs
1 cup molasses
3 1/2 cups flour
1 1/2 tsp. soda
1 tsp. salt

1 tsp. cloves
2 tsp. cinnamon
1/2 tsp. nutmeg
1 cup strong coffee
1 cup currents
1 cup raisins

Cream lard, sugar and eggs and beat quite light. Add molasses. Sift flour with soda, salt and spices. Sift three times. Add the sifted flour gradually to the butter egg mixture with the coffee. Add the currents and raisins. These quantities make 2 loaf cakes.
Bake in a very moderate oven 45 to 60 minutes. The cake is better if kept 5 weeks before cutting.

Nancy Piatkowski
Documentary Heritage Program
Buffalo, NY

WATERMELON CAKE

8 Tbsp. butter
1 cup sugar
2/3 cup milk
3 cups flour
3 tsp. baking powder
2 eggs

1/2 tsp. almond extract
1/2 tsp. vanilla extract
Red food coloring
1/2 cup raisins
Green food color

White part: 4 Tbsp. butter, 1/2 cup sugar, 1/3 cup milk, 1 1/2 cups flour, 1 1/2 tsp. baking powder, 2 egg whites, beaten light and almond extract. Pink part: use same quantities, taking yolks of the eggs, vanilla extract and enough red food coloring to make a pretty pink color, add raisins. Line a long narrow pan with waxed paper and pour white mixture into it and the pink over that.

(con't next page)

WATERMELON CAKE (CON'T)

Bake as a layer cake in a moderate oven as for a layer cake. When cool make a white icing and color it a pale green with the green food coloring. Cut into strips to serve.

Nancy Piatkowski
Documentary Heritage Program
Buffalo, NY

FOURTH OF JULY CAKE

Use the same recipe as given for the Watermelon Cake, leaving out the raisins in the pink part.
For a third or blue part, use:

1/4 cup butter
1/2 cup sugar
1 cup flour

1 tsp. baking powder
1 egg
Blueberry or loganberry
    juice

Mix ingredients adding enough juice for cake batter consistency. Add more red coloring to the pink layer. Put together with white icing, having red cake at the bottom, then white layer and blue on top. Decorate with tiny flags.

Nancy Piatkowski
Documentary Heritage Program
Buffalo, NY

OLD TIME BISHOPS BREAD
OR
DATE & NUT BARS

2 eggs
1/2 cup sugar
1/2 tsp. vanilla
1/2 cup flour

1/2 tsp. salt
1 cup chopped nuts
2 cups cut up dates
Confectioners sugar

Beat eggs until foamy. Beat in sugar and vanilla. Stir in flour and salt. Mix in nuts and dates. Pour into 8" greased square pan.
Bake at 350° for 25-30 minutes until crust looks dull. Cool slightly and cut into squares while warm. Dip in sifted confectioners sugar.
These store well. I always make these 2 days ahead. This recipe is from the turn of the century from Jennie Bobzin Dunlop.

Donna May Barnes

CARROT COOKIES
from Lockport Union Sun & Journal, Jan. 3, 1918

1 cup brown sugar
1/3 cup molasses
1/2 cup fat
1 cup carrots, boiled & mashed
3/4 cup raisins
1 egg, beaten
1 1/2 cups flour

2 tsp. baking powder
1/2 tsp. salt
1 tsp. vanilla
1/4 tsp. cinnamon
1/4 tsp. cloves
1/4 tsp. nutmeg

Mix the ingredients well and drop the dough by spoonfuls in greased pans.
Bake the cookies in a moderate oven.

Ann Bruski

(166)

MOTHER PAPKE'S CHRISTMAS COOKIES

1 pt. molasses
1 pt. dark Karo syrup
1 lb. lard
1 pt. buttermilk

1 lb. almonds, ground*
1 Tbsp. baking soda
8 1/2-10 cups flour

Slowly boil for 10 minutes the following ingredients: molasses, Karo and lard. Cool to room temperature. Then add buttermilk, nuts, baking soda and mix thoroughly. Stir in the flour. Keep adding the flour until you have reached at least 8 1/2 cups. Try to stir in all 10 if you have the strength in your arms, if not stop when you give up!
Here's the SECRET...let the mixture stand in a cool spot for 10 days! Roll out dough to about 1/2" thick and cut into rounds about 3" in diameter.
Bake at 375° for 8-10 minutes. Frost with a glaze made of confectioners sugar. You can place a whole nut on top. You can add cinnamon to the cookie mixture if desired, we don't. *You may also substitute walnuts for the almonds but almonds are the tradition.
Note: This is an old time Town of Pendleton tradition at Christmas dating back 150 years! The recipe is credited to "Mother Papke" who made the cookies every year at the holiday season for her family and friends.

Terry J. Miller

JUMBLES
from *The Cook Not Mad; or Rational Cookery*
Being a Collection of Original and Selected Receipts 1831

Half a pound of butter, half a pound of sugar, three quarters of a pound of flour, two eggs, mix and roll in sugar and nutmeg; to be dropped on tins to bake.

(Con't next page)

JUMBLES (CON'T)
Modern Conversion

1 cup butter
1 1/2~2 cups flour
2 eggs

1 cup brown sugar
Sugar & nutmeg

Cream butter and brown sugar. Beat egg whites and yolks separately. Add each to butter mixture. Slowly mix in flour. This should be a very soft dough. Roll into balls and roll balls in sugar and nutmeg.
Bake at 350° on a greased cookie sheet for 7~10 minutes. Biscuits should not change color.

Compliments of Dundern Castle,
Hamilton, Ontario, Canada

CIVIL WAR SUGAR COOKIES

2 cups sugar
1 cup butter
3 eggs, well beaten
1/4 tsp. baking soda, dissolved
   in 1 Tbsp. boiling water

1 tsp. nutmeg
1/2 tsp. cloves
4 cups flour

Cream butter and sugar. Add the eggs and baking soda dissolved in boiling water. Mix thoroughly. Stir in nutmeg and cloves. Add flour gradually to make a dough just stiff enough to roll. Roll out on lightly floured board and cut out with a large cookie cutter (bottom of a 1# coffee can works well). Place on a lightly greased baking sheet and put a raisin or current on each cookie. Dust heavily with sugar.
Bake at 375° for 10~12 minutes. Yield: 2 1/2 dozen.
These cookies have a solid, old fashioned texture and flavoring is a nice surprise.

Joan Crea

GRANDMA'S MOLASSES COOKIES

2/3 cup cooking oil
1 cup sugar
1 cup molasses
1 medium egg, well beaten
3 tsp. soda dissolved in 1/2 c.
  boiling water

5 1/2 cups flour
3 tsp. cream of tartar
1 tsp. ginger
1 tsp. cinnamon
1/2 tsp. salt

Beat together oil, sugar and molasses. Add egg and soda dissolved in boiling water. Sift all dry ingredients together and add to the rest. Mix well and chill. Roll out 1/4" thick on floured and sugared surface. Cut cookies.
Bake at 400° for 8-10 minutes. Watch carefully!
This recipe is at least 150 years old!

Marion James
Taken from Niagara Falls DAR Heritage Recipes-1990
with permission-compiled by Ann Bruski

MOM'S OLD FASHIONED SOFT SUGAR COOKIES
Lula Gerard Roberts -- Frances Roberts Zehner

3 1/4 cups sifted flour
1 tsp. soda
1/2 tsp. salt
1/2 cup soft butter or margarine
1/2 cup thick sour cream

1 cup sugar
1 egg, unbeaten
1 1/2 tsp. vanilla or 1 tsp.
  nutmeg

(con't next page)

SOFT SUGAR COOKIES (CON'T)

Sift together, flour, soda and salt. Combine in large bowl, butter, sugar, egg and flavoring. Beat for 2 minutes. Add sour cream and then flour mixture gradually while beating, about 2 minutes. Scrape bowl as necessary. Roll out on lightly floured surface to 1/4" thickness. Sprinkle with sugar and roll it in lightly. Cut with floured cutter. Place on greased cookie sheet. Put a raisin, nutmeat or piece of gum drop in center if you like.
Bake at 400° about 12 minutes until golden brown. Cool. Makes about 2 1/2 dozen cookies. 100 year old recipe!

Anna Zehner Bruski
Taken from Niagara Falls DAR Heritage Recipes~1990
with permission~compiled by Ann Bruski

NUT MINTS

1 1/4 cups sifted confectioners
 sugar
1/4 cup Eagle Brand sweetened
 condensed milk

Red food coloring
Green food coloring
Walnut or Pecan halves
Peppermint extract

Put confectioners sugar into a medium sized bowl. Blend in condensed milk. Add peppermint extract to taste. Mix with wooden spoon until smooth and creamy. Take half the mixture and put it into a second bowl for adding food color. Tint one half of the mixture a delicate pink with red food coloring. Tint the other half a delicate green with green food coloring. Take a small teaspoonful at a time and roll it into a small ball between the palms of your hands which first have been dusted with confectioner's sugar. Place the balls on wax paper lined cookie sheets and allow to set.*
Top each with a nut half and let dry. Turn over once to dry the bottoms. makes 2 dozen.
*Optional: flatten a little with the bottom of a glass.
These are very similar to the butter creams that my mother made at Christmas time.

Ann Bruski

MASHED POTATO CANDY

1 potato, boiled and mashed   1 tsp.vanilla or other
Pinch of salt   flavoring
Confectioner's sugar

Mix potato, salt and flavoring together. Add enough confectioner's sugar to mold. Shape and decorate as desired with coconut, nuts or chocolate.
Note: a large potato might use as much as 2 lbs. confectioner's sugar to mold in and take up the moisture!
This is an old Pennsylvania Dutch recipe!

Isabel Hobba
Sylvia Konopka
Taken from Niagara Falls DAR Heritage Recipes-1990
with permission-compiled by Ann Bruski

CRANBERRY SALAD

1 pkg. fresh cranberries	2 cups water
2 cups sugar	2 boxes cherry gelatin
2 cups chopped celery	1 cup chopped nuts

Cook cranberries in water and sugar until cranberries pop open. Remove from heat. Add the cherry gelatin powder and mix well. Pour into mold or dish. Cool. Add celery and nuts.

Ann Bruski

CRANBERRY~ORANGE RELISH

1 lb. cranberries	2 oranges
2 cups sugar	

Wash and sort cranberries. Cut oranges into sections. Do not peel. Remove seeds. Put berries and oranges through meat grinder using the fine blade. (Modern version would be to use a food processor.) Mix with sugar. Chill before serving. Relish can be put into container and covered with paraffin.
Both my grandmothers liked and used this recipe at holiday times!

Phila Brooks Ibaugh
Taken from Niagara Falls DAR Heritage Recipes~1990
with permission~compiled by Ann Bruski

(172)

APPLE BROWN BETTY
from *The Niagara Falls Gazette* -Jan. 11, 1932

2 qts. diced tart apples
1 qt. bread crumbs,
   lightly toasted
1 1/4 cups sugar

1 tsp. cinnamon
1/4 tsp. salt
1/4 cup melted butter

Grease a baking dish and place in it a layer of crumbs, then a layer of apples, and some of the sugar, cinnamon and salt, which have been mixed together. Repeat until all the ingredients are used, saving sufficient crumbs for the top. Pour the melted fat over the top layer of crumbs and cover. Bake for 30-45 minutes or until the apples are soft. Toward the last, remove the cover and allow the top to brown. Serve with (or without) top milk or sauce.

Donald E. Loker

APPLE CRISP

8 or more apples
1/2 cup white sugar
2 Tbsp. lemon juice

1 cup flour
1/2 cup brown sugar
1/2 cup margarine

Combine flour, brown sugar and margarine until crumbly. Slice apples and mix with sugar and lemon juice. Place in a pan and top with the crumb mixture.
Bake at 325° for 50 minutes or until done.

Betty Moot
Taken from Niagara Falls DAR Heritage Recipes-1990
with permission-compiled by Ann Bruski

(173)

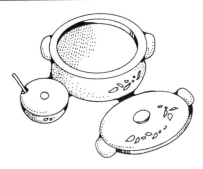

BAKED INDIAN PUDDING
from *The Niagara Falls Gazette*-Jan.11, 1932

1 quart milk
1/3 cup yellow cornmeal
1 tsp. salt

1/2 cups molasses
1/2-1 tsp. ginger

Cook the milk, cornmeal and salt in a double boiler for 20 minutes. Add the molasses and ginger. Pour into a greased baking dish.
Bake in a very moderate oven for 2 hours.

Donald E. Loker

LEMON CUPS

1 1/2 cups sugar
1/2 cup flour
1/4 tsp. salt
3 Tbsp. melted butter
Juice of 1 lemon

1 lemon rind, grated
5 well beaten egg yolks
5 well beaten egg yolks
2 cups scalded milk

Combine sugar, flour, salt, lemon juice and rind. Add beaten egg yolks. Add scalded milk and butter. Fold in beaten egg whites. Pour into greased custard cups.
Bake at 325° in a pan of hot water for 45 minutes. Finished, it turns into a light cake topping and a lemon pudding below. Tastes refreshing!
Recipe from my mother-in-law, Helen Cadman Bruski.

Ann Bruski

(174)

SHOO~FLY PIE

1 9" pie shell
3/4 cup flour
1/2 cup dark brown sugar
1/4 tsp. salt
1 egg yolk, well beaten
1 1/2 tsp. baking soda

1/2 tsp. cinnamon
1/8 tsp. nutmeg
1/8 tsp. ginger
2 Tbsp. shortening
1/2 cup dark molasses
3/4 cup boiling water

Combine beaten egg yolk with molasses. Stir in baking soda which has been dissolved in the boiling water and allowed to bubble up. Mix together dry ingredients with shortening. Alternate layers of liquid and dry ingredients into pie shell ending with the crumbs on top.
Bake at 450° for 10 minutes until the edges brown, then reduce heat to 350 for 20 minutes longer or until firm. This is a favorite of mine. The pie is so named because it is sweet and the flies have to be shooed away!

Isabel Korman Hobba
Taken from Niagara Falls DAR Heritage Recipes~1990
with permission~compiled by Ann Bruski

STEAMED APRICOT PUDDING
from *The Niagara Falls Gazette*~Jan. 11, 1932

1/2 lb. dried apricots
1/2 cup suet
1 egg
1/4 tsp. salt

1 1/2 cup soft-wheat flour
1/2 cup sugar
2 tsp. baking powder
1/2 cup milk

Wash the apricots, chop fine and mix with 2 Tbsp. of the flour. Sift the remaining flour with the baking powder and salt. Cream the fat, add the sugar and well beaten egg. Add alternately with the milk to the sifted dry ingredients. Stir in the apricots. Pour into a greased mold. Cover and steam for 2 hours. Serve with a vanilla sauce.

Donald E. Loker

STEAMED CARROT PUDDING

1 cup grated carrots	2 cups flour
1 cup ground suet	1 tsp. baking soda
1 cup grated raw potato	1 tsp. salt
1 cup raisins	1 tsp. cinnamon
1 cup dried currents	1 tsp. nutmeg
1 cup sugar	

Mix all ingredients together. Even if mixture is very dry, do not add any liquid! Steam for 3 hours. A double boiler works just as well if you don't have a steamer, but make sure the water in the bottom pan doesn't boil away.

Serve with your favorite lemon or hard sauce. My grandmother, Mary Fisher, made this when I was a small child and I haven't missed making it for Christmas dinner for 37 years. The recipe came with her from England in 1912.

Patricia O. Few

CHIPPED BEEF NOODLE CASSEROLE

10 oz. noodles
1/8 cup butter
1 cup chopped celery
5 oz. chipped beef
3/4 tsp. celery salt

2 cans Campbell's celery
   soup
2 1/2 cups milk
1/2 cup dry fine bread
   crumbs

Cook noodles until tender and drain. Melt butter in large skillet. Add celery and cook slowly until tender. Add beef, soup and milk. Add seasoning and blend mixture. Add noodles and stir. Pour into buttered casserole and cover with bread crumbs. Dot with butter. Cover dish. Bake at 350° for 1 hour. This recipe was found in a magazine by her mother in the 1930's.

Geraldine Miller
Taken from Niagara Falls DAR Heritage Recipes~1990
with permission~compiled by Ann Bruski

GROUND BEEF BROILED ON TOAST
from *The Niagara Falls Gazette*-Jan. 11, 1932

1 lb. ground raw beef
8 slices bread

Butter
Salt & pepper to taste

Toast the bread on one side. Butter the untoasted side. Spread to the edge with a layer of raw ground beef. Dot with butter and broil under a flame for about 5 minutes. Season with salt and pepper and serve at once with a garnish of parsley or pickles.

Donald E. Loker

SCOTCH COLLOPS

1 lb. ground beef
2 cups water
Salt & pepper

Onion to taste
1/2 cup milk

Place meat in a pan. Add water. Stir until there are no lumps. Add onion and seasonings. Simmer 10 minutes. Add thickening of milk. Serve with noodles or mashed potatoes.

Clara Lockie
Taken from Niagara Falls DAR Heritage Recipes~1990
with permission~compiled by Ann Bruski

STEAMED BEEF STEW
from *The Niagara Falls Gazette*~April 21, 1899

Set a tin pan in boiling water. Cut into thin slices 1 1/2 pounds of the round of beef. Lay in the stewpan and cover with a gravy as follows: 3 Tbsp. of melted butter, one of walnut catsup, 1 tsp. of vinegar, one of mixed mustard, one of current jelly, 1/8 of a tsp. salt and 2 shakes of pepper. Keep the water boiling constantly and steam 30 minutes.

Donald E. Loker, author
The News of the Day...Yesterday

(178)

YANKEE HAM & BEAN SOUP

2 cups dried pea, navy or
   lima beans
1 ham bone
1 bay leaf
3 tsp. salt
1 cup grated carrots

8 cups cold water
1/4 cup ketchup
2 tsp. minced onion
1/4 tsp. black pepper
1/8 tsp. garlic powder

Soak beans overnight. Add ham bone, bay leaf and salt.
Cover and simmer all day. Remove bone and 1/2 cup of the
beans. Put remaining beans through course sieve. Combine
beans, bean puree, carrots, minced onion and ketchup.
Cook till carrots are tender, about 15 minutes. Add pepper
and garlic powder. Cut meat off the bone and add.
Makes about 10 servings.

Betty Allen
Taken from Niagara Falls DAR Heritage Recipes-1990
with permission-compiled by Ann Bruski

CURRIED CHICKEN OR SHRIMP

4 boneless chicken breasts or
   1 lb. large, cleaned shrimp
2 Tbsp. butter
3/4 cup chopped onion
1/2 cup chopped celery
1 clove garlic, minced

2 tsp. curry powder
1 bay leaf
1 apple, peeled & diced
1 banana, diced
2 tsp. tomato paste
1 1/2 cups chicken broth

Sauté onion, celery and garlic in butter until tender.
Sprinkle with curry powder. Add bay leaf, apple and
banana. Add chicken broth and tomato paste. Stir to blend.
Add chicken and simmer for 20 minutes.
When making curried shrimp follow the above directions
but only cook shrimp for 5 minutes.

Onalee Carlisle
Taken from Niagara Falls DAR Heritage Recipes-1990
with permission-compiled by Ann Bruski

SAVORY CHICKEN & RICE
Special dish served by Alice Angel Outwater
and Dr. Samuel Outwater at 215 Niagara St. Lockport, NY
now the home of the Niagara County Historical Society!

Once I watched Great Aunt Alice cooking. You might not be
able to follow her recipe but it went something like this:
Half fill medium size black cast iron sauce pan with hot
water. Add rice to proper level. Simmer on back of coal
stove. Add chive tips from plant on rear windowsill.
While rice bubbles, fry cut-up, freshly eviscerated and
cleaned chicken in iron skillet. I think she called it a
spider. Turn chicken as needed. When fork pokes it
properly, sprinkle a pinch of salt over chicken. Add a little
pinch or two from each of 3 salt cups on the left hand end
of the spice rack (unknown seasoning!). Add a small scoop
of flour and stir under chicken. Add hot water a little at a
time as it thickens.
Place rice in a warm fluted bowl. Add chicken and gravy,
serve and say "grace" and enjoy!
My mother was Ada Grace Adkins Buck, daughter of Uncle
Sam's sister, Elizabeth Outwater Adkins, So I am Uncle
Sam's grand niece.

Ada Elizabeth Buck Reynolds

CLAM PIE

1 pt. clams or 1 can clams	1 Tbsp. flour
Salt & pepper	Pastry for a 2 crust pie
Butter	

Put clams through a food chopper. With the clam liquor
mix flour diluted with a little cold water and add to the
clams. Season with salt and pepper. Line a deep pie plate
with pastry, pour in clams and put on the top crust. Dot
small pieces of butter over top crust.
Bake in a hot oven about 20 minutes.

Nancy Piatkowski
Documentary Heritage Program
Buffalo, NY

CREAMED OYSTERS
from *The Niagara Falls Gazette* - April 22, 1899

Allow to each pint of oysters a Tbsp. of butter. Melt the butter, throw in the oysters and mix thoroughly. Moisten a Tbsp. of flour in a little milk, then add half a pint. Pour this over the oysters and bring to the boiling point. Season with salt and pepper.

By adding the yolks of 2 eggs and a Tbsp. of chopped parsley, you may convert them into fricassee of oysters.

"Au natural", the oysters are simply thrown into a hot chafing dish and when boiling, salt, pepper and butter to taste are added.

Donald E. Loker, author
The News of the Day...Yesterday

LOBSTER WIGGLE

3 Tbsp. butter
3 Tbsp. flour
1 cup canned peas
1/8 tsp. pepper

2 cups milk or cream
1 cup canned lobster
1/2 tsp. salt

Melt butter and add flour. When bubbling, gradually add the milk or cream, stirring until thickened. Add the lobster broken into small pieces and the drained peas. Season with the salt and pepper. Serve on buttered toast.

Note: Cold, cooked chicken or shrimp may be used in the same way. Shreds of green pepper may be used instead of the peas.

Nancy Piatkowski
Documentary Heritage Program
Buffalo, NY

(181)

CARROT LOAF
Lockport *Union, Sun & Journal*-Jan. 3, 1918

1 1/2 cupfuls ground carrot
1 cupful boiled rice
1 cupful ground peanuts
1 cupful milk
1 egg
Salt & pepper

2 Tbsp. minced green
peppers
3 Tbsp. minced bacon or
other fat
1 Tbsp. onion juice
1/2 tsp. mustard

Mix the ingredient in the order given (column 1, then column 2).
Bake the loaf in a moderate oven for 1 hour. Serve it with a tomato sauce if desired. This loaf is a heavy, full-bodied meal. Different, but good!

Ann Bruski

CAYENNE CHEESES
from *The book of Household management* ~ 1862

1/2 lb. butter
1/2 lb. flour
1/2 lb. grated cheese

1 tsp. cayenne
1/3 tsp. salt
Water

Rub the butter in the flour. Add the grated cheese, cayenne and salt and mix well together. Moisten with sufficient water to make the whole into a paste. Roll out and cut into fingers about 4 inches in length.
Bake them in a moderate oven until a very light colour and serve very hot.

Modern Conversion

1 cup butter
1/3 tsp. salt
2 cups grated cheese

1 1/2 cups flour
1/3 tsp. cayenne pepper
Water

Prepare as above. Use more cayenne if you prefer spicy.
Bake at 350° for 12~15 minutes.

Compliments of Dundern Castle
Hamilton, Ontario, Canada

MACARONI AU GRATIN
from *The Niagara Falls Gazette*-Apr. 20, 1899

(Note: This recipe is located with side dishes because this is where we now use it, or even as a main dish...but read on:)

This recipe is for dessert and is a dainty dish to serve as a cheese plate. Use 1/8 of a pound of macaroni broken into two inch pieces. Boil till tender, but unbroken. Put in a small, buttered gratiner one layer of macaroni and a layer of equally thick grated cheese with the juice of 1/4th of a lemon. Fill to level with thick cream.
Bake in a very hot oven 10 minutes. It should be served almost hot after the sweet.

Donald E. Loker

DEVILED EGGS

12 hard-cooked eggs
1/8 cup prepared mustard
1/4 tsp. salt
1/3 tsp. paprika

1/8 cup drained, sweet
  pickle relish
1/3 cup mayonnaise

Slice eggs in half lengthwise. Remove yolks carefully. In a bowl blend yolks, mustard, salt, relish and mayonnaise thoroughly. Overstuff the whites with the mixture. Sprinkle with paprika. Serve immediately or place in refrigerator to chill.
A very old heritage recipe and one that I liked as a child.

Melody Genovesia
Taken from Niagara Falls DAR Heritage Recipes-1990
with permission-compiled by Ann Bruski

(183)

PICKLED EGGS

16 eggs
1 qt. vinegar
1/2 oz. black pepper

1/2 oz. ginger
1/2 oz. Jamaica pepper

Boil the eggs for 12 minutes, then dip them into cold water. Take off the shells. Put the vinegar, with the pepper and ginger, into a stewpan and let simmer for 10 minutes. Now place the eggs in a jar. Pour over them the vinegar &c. boiling hot. When cold, tie them down with bladder to exclude the air. This pickle will be ready for use in a month.

This should be made about Easter, as at this time eggs are plentiful and cheap. A store of pickled eggs will be found very useful and ornamental in serving with many first and second course dishes.

Modern Conversion

16 eggs
1 Tbsp. allspice
1 Tbsp. ginger

4 cups vinegar
1 Tbsp. whole black
    peppercorns

Hard boil the eggs for 12 minutes. When cold, peel the eggs. Simmer the vinegar and spices together for 10 minutes. Place eggs in sterilized jar and pour the boiling vinegar over. Seal. Enjoy in 1 month's time.

Compliments of Dundern Castle
Hamilton, Ontario, Canada

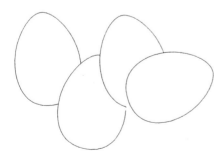

(184)

POTATO RISSOLES
from *The Book of Household Management* -1862

Mashed potatoes, salt and pepper to taste; when liked a very little minced parsley, egg and bread crumbs.

Boil and mash the potatoes. Add a seasoning of pepper and salt, and, when like, a little minced parsley. Roll the potatoes into small balls. Cover them with egg and bread crumbs and fry in hot lard for about 10 minutes. Let them drain before the fire. Dish them on a napkin and serve.
The flavour of these rissoles may be very much increased by adding finely minced tongue or ham, or even onions, when these are liked.

Modern Conversion

Mashed potatoes	Salt & pepper to taste
Parsley (optional)	1 egg
Bread crumbs	

Roll the mashed potatoes into small balls. Dip into egg and roll in breadcrumbs. Fry in lightly oiled pan until brown.

Compliments of Dundern Castle
Hamilton, Ontario, Canada

SCALLOPED POTATOES

3 Tbsp. margarine or butter	2 Tbsp. flour
1 tsp. salt	Pepper to taste
Paprika	2 cups milk
5-6 cups potatoes, thinly sliced	Minced onion

(Con't next page)

SCALLOPED POTATOES (CON'T)

Melt 2 Tbsp. margarine in large saucepan. Stir in flour, salt and pepper to taste. Add a few shakes of paprika. Gradually stir in milk and cook, stirring constantly, until sauce boils and thickens slightly. Add sliced potatoes and minced onion to taste. (2 tsp. onion powder could be added to sauce in place of raw onion.) Heat, stirring to mix thoroughly. Turn into a baking dish, dot with 1 Tbsp. margarine or butter.
Bake at 350° until done and golden brown, about 45 minutes depending on type of baking dish used. Sprinkle with paprika, parsley or chives, as desired. Makes 5-7 servings. This recipe can be doubled easily.
Potatoes are a big part of our basic heritage!

Isabel Hobba
Taken from Niagara Falls DAR Heritage Recipes-1990
with permission-compiled by Ann Bruski

SUCCOTASH
Narragansett-American Indian for a dish consisting of
lima beans and kernels of corn cooked together!

When America was discovered, the Indians were cultivating corn (misickquatash), their favorite food. Columbus is said to have carried the first grains of it to Europe and the Indians taught the colonists how to grow corn and prepare it. At harvest time even the braves of the tribe joined the squaws to help bring in and husk the corn.

Jean Laird
Taken from Niagara Falls DAR Heritage Recipes-1990
with permission-compiled by Ann Bruski

(186)

CRANBERRY SALAD

1 pkg. fresh cranberries	2 cups water
2 cups sugar	2 boxes cherry gelatin
2 cups chopped celery	1 cup chopped nuts

In saucepan, put cranberries, water and sugar and cook until cranberries pop open. Remove from heat. Add gelatin powder and mix well. Pour into mold or dish. Cool. Add celery and nuts and chill until set.

Ann Bruski

CRANBERRY~ORANGE RELISH

1 lb. cranberries	2 oranges
2 cups sugar	

Wash and sort cranberries. Cut oranges into sections. Do not peel! Remove seeds. Put berries and orange through a meat grinder using the fine blade. (Modern version would be to use a food processor.) Mix with sugar. Chill well before serving.
Relish can be put into a container and covered with paraffin.
Both of my Grandmother's liked and used this recipe at holiday times.

Phila Brooks Ibaugh
Taken from Niagara Falls DAR Heritage Recipes-1990
with permission~compiled by Ann Bruski

WALDORF SALAD

2 cups diced red apples
1/2 cup chopped walnuts
Lettuce

1 cup diced celery
6 Tbsp. mayonnaise or
salad dressing

Mix ingredients lightly with salad dressing. Serve on lettuce cups. Garnish each salad with chopped nut meats, a Maraschino cherry or 1 tsp. red jelly.
Optional additions: bananas, pineapple, mandarin oranges.
I remember my mother making this salad.

Vada Cessna
Taken from Niagara Falls DAR Heritage Recipes-1990
with permission-compiled by Ann Bruski

FOR SPRAINS

1 egg white
1 Tbsp. Epsom Salts
1 Tbsp. honey
Double the recipe if a larger quantity is needed!

Beat together very, very well. Apply to sprain area or on gauze type cloth. Wrap sprain area with this cloth. Put a towel on top of that. Allow to stay on as long as you can.
This has been a family treatment recipe for over 50 years. It was given to us by Therapist Ray Barclay of South Bend, Indiana. I can personally attest that it works on ankle sprains!

Anna Zehner Bruski
Taken from Niagara Falls DAR Heritage
with permission-compiled by Ann Bruski

RECIPES & NOTES

RECIPES & NOTES

READ	SEE	THAT	ME?
DOWN	WILL	I	LOVE
AND	YOU	LOVE	YOU
UP	AND	YOU.	DO

Virginia Strablow

ANSWER:

Read down and up and you will see that I love you. Do you love me?

HINTS FROM THE PAST

An Iron Skillet should be washed with steel wool and soap. Food will stick and a pan will rust if detergent is used. Once a year rub a bit of edible oil in the pan to help keep it from rusting!

Christa Caldwell

....

All Cooking Utensils, including ironware, should be washed outside and inside with hot, soapy water, rinsed in clean hot water and wiped dry with a dry towel. A soapy or greasy dishcloth should never be used for this purpose!

....

To Clean Decanters: Cut some raw potatoes in pieces and put them in the bottle with a little cold water. Rinse and the bottle will look very clean!

....

To Remove the Odor of Onion from fish-kettle and saucepans in which they have been cooked, put wood ashes or sal soda, potash or lye and fill with water. Let stand on the stove until water boils, then wash in hot suds and rinse well!

....

To Keep Milk Sweet: Put in pan a spoonful of grated horseradish. It will keep the milk sweet for days!

....

To Prevent the Odor of Boiling Ham or Cabbage: Throw red pepper pods or a few bits of charcoal into the pan they are cooked in!

HINTS FROM THE PAST

To Make Tough Meat Tender: Lay it a few minutes in a strong vinegar water!

....

Never Allow Fresh Meat to remain in paper. It absorbs the juices!

....

How to Tell Good Eggs: If you desire to be certain that your eggs are good and fresh, put them in water; if the butts turn up, they are not fresh. This is an infallible rule to distinguish a good egg from a bad one.

....

Storing Vinegar: Never keep vinegar or yeast in stone crocks or jugs. Their acid attacks the glazing, which is said to be poisonous. Glass for either is better!

....

Poison Water: Water boiled in galvanized iron becomes poisonous, and cold water passed through zinc-lined iron pipes should never be used for cooking or drinking! Hot water for cooking should never be taken from hot water pipes; keep a supply heated in kettles.

HINTS FROM THE PAST

For a Sick Headache: Put the feet into hot mustard water, lay a cold wet cloth on the stomach with dry flannel over it, and swallow a few spoonfuls of lemon juice!

....

A Cure For Rheumatism: Lemon juice is recommended as a certain cure for acute rheumatism. It is given in quantities of a Tbsp. to twice the quantity of cold water, with sugar, every hour. The effect of the lemon juice is almost instantaneous.

....

To Relieve a Sore Throat: Take the foot of the stocking warm from the foot, and pin it around the throat and wear it all night.

....

Asthma: A cup of strong coffee will often give relief, although it is apt to act upon the nerves of a weak patient.

....

Nosebleed Cure: Roll up a piece of paper and pass it up under the upper lip. In obstinate cases blow a little gum Arabic up the nostrils through a quill which will immediately stop the discharge. The bleeding can mostly b e stopped by making the patient raise both arms above his head, and hold them there for some time. As a last resort, take lint or cotton wool, soak it in a solution of alum and plug up both nostrils.

HINTS FROM THE PAST

To Drive Away Bedbugs: Take the whites of 4 eggs and 10 cents' worth of quick silver and beat together until a stiff froth. Take a feather, dip in and apply to the bedstead.

....

An Ant Trap: Procure a large sponge, wash it well, and press it dry, which will leave the cells quite open. Sprinkle over it some fine, white sugar, and place it near where the ants are most troublesome. They will soon collect upon the sponge and take up their abode in the cells. It is then only necessary to dip the sponge in scalding water, which will ash them out "clean dead" by ten thousands. Put on more sugar, and set the trap for a new haul. This process will soon clear the house of every ant, uncle and progeny.

....

An Agreeable Disinfectant: Sprinkle fresh ground coffee on a shovel of hot coals, or burn sugar on hot coals. Vinegar boiled with myrrh, sprinkled on the floor and furniture of a sick room, are excellent deodorizers.

....

To Ventilate a Room: Place a pitcher of cold water on a table in your room and it will absorb all the gases with which the room is filled from the respiration of those eating or sleeping. Very few realize how important such purification is for the health of the family, or, indeed, understand or realize that there can be any impurity in the rooms; yet in a few hours a pitcher or pail of cold water (the colder the more effective) will make the air of a room pure, but the water will be entirely unfit for use.

HINTS FROM THE PAST

To Brighten Carpets: Carpets after the dust has been beaten out may be brightened by scattering upon them cornmeal mixed with salt and then seeping it off. Mix salt and meal in equal proportions. Carpets should be thoroughly beaten on the wrong side first and then on the right side, after which spots may be removed by the use of ox-gall or ammonia and water.

....

To Erase Discoloration on Stone China: Dishes and cups that are used for baking custards, puddings, etc., that require scouring, may be easily cleaned by rubbing with a damp cloth dipped in whiting or "Sapolio", then washed as usual.

....

To Remove Ink, Wine, or Fruit Stains: Saturate well in tomato juice. It is also an excellent thing to remove stains from the hands.

....

To Set Colors in Washable Goods: Soak them previous to washing in a water in which is allowed a Tbsp. of ox-gall to a gallon of water.

....

To Prevent Lamp-wicks from Smoking: Soak them in vinegar and then dry them thoroughly.

....

Never Use Water Alert: Never use water which has stood in a lead pipe overnight. Not less that a bucketful should be allowed to run.

HINTS FROM THE PAST

Furniture Cleaner: 1 quart hot water, 3 Tbsp. Boiled linseed oil, 1 Tbsp. Turpentine. Mix and keep hot in a double boiler. Apply with a damp cloth and rub with the grain. Polish with a soft dry cloth.

. . . .

Furniture Polish: 1 Tbsp. Sweet oil, 1 Tbsp. Lemon juice and 1 Tbsp. Cornstarch. Mix and apply with a soft cloth.

. . . .

To Take Off Starch & Rust From Irons: Tie a piece of yellow beeswax in a rag, and when the iron is almost hot enough for use, rub it with the beeswax quickly, and then with a clean course cloth.

. . . .

To Clean Silk and Make It New: Put an old kid glove in a pint of cold water. Let it boil until the water is reduced to one-half the quantity. Sponge the silk with this water on the right side, and iron it on the wrong side. This will make old silks and ribbons look like new.

. . . .

Cleaning Jewelry: For cleaning jewelry there is nothing better than ammonia and water. If very dull or dirty, rub a little soap on a soft brush and brush the jewelry in this wash, rinse in cold water, dry first in an old handkerchief and then rub with buck or chamois skin. Their freshness and brilliancy when thus cleaned cannot be surpassed by any compound used by jewelers.

HINTS FROM THE PAST

To Preserve Bouquets: Put a little saltpeter in the water you use for your bouquets, and the flowers will live for a fortnight.

....

To Preserve Creaking of Bedsteads: If a bedstead creaks at each movement of the sleeper, remove the slats, and wrap the ends of each in old newspapers.

....

To Preserve Brooms: Dip them for a minute or two in a kettle of boiling suds once a week and they will last much longer, making them tough and pliable. A carpet wears much longer swept with a broom cared for in this manner.

RECIPES & NOTES

RECIPES & NOTES

INDEX

(199)

(200)

TASTES
of the
PAST & PRESENT

Edited by
Patricia O. Few

A very special thank you to the
community of Niagara County
and the membership of
the Niagara County Historical Society
for their contributions to this
year 2000 project!

1st Printing

The Niagara County Historical Society, Inc.
215 Niagara Street
Lockport, New York 14094
Incorporated
1957
ISBN 1-878233-26-2

A BIT ABOUT TASTES OF THE PAST

Scattered throughout the pages of this book are recipes from cookbooks dating as far back as 1861 and recipes dating from 1791! They will be bordered and in *italics!* These recipes are in addition to the Special Heritage Section.

A special thank you to Donna Barnes, Mary Newhard and NCHS for the loan of these books. They are:

"The American Practical Cookery-Book", c.1861 J.W.Bradley
"A Book of Recipes" spanning 1791-1956, Farny & Wurlitzer
"Gold Medal Cookbook" c.1909, Washburn-Crosby
"The Model Cook Book", c.1900-Title page missing
"Recipe Book of Jennie Bobzin Dunlap", handwritten c.1915.

You will note when you read these recipes that some of the measurements are a little strange. Follow them exactly as written. It is also important to remember that in the era that most of these recipes were used, the ovens were either open fireplaces or wood stoves or ovens without thermometers.

The following instructions were taken from one of the above cookbooks...

HEATING OVENS: This must be done by experience and observation. There is a difference in wood in giving out heat and a big difference in the construction of ovens. As a general rule, a smart fire for an hour is long enough for bread and pies. In order to test the heat of an oven, throw in a little flour and shut the oven door for a minute. If it scorches black immediately it is too hot, if it only browns it is about right!

An oven of the best make and construction can be made, by careful attention and a little judicious management, to do five successive bakings with one heating...first the bread, then the puddings, then pies, then gingerbread and then custard, which will bake sufficiently by leaving in longer!

AND IN ANOTHER BOOK: Conversions for recipes that lack baking temperatures:

A Slow Oven = 250° to 350°

A Moderate Oven = 350° to 400°

A Hot Oven = 400° to 450°

HAVE A GOOD TIME TRYING THE HERITAGE RECIPES!